Looking at HISTORIC BUILDINGS in Holland

Looking at HISTORIC

BUILDINGS
n Holland

. P. Smaal (compiler and editor-in-chief)
nd G. Berends W. F. Denslagen M. E. Doets
. L. van Groningen J. T. M. Gunneweg
. R. G. Hofstee G. H. Keunen L. Prins
. Roosegaarde Bisschop F. W. van Voorden

With the exception of Chapter 7, which has been specially written, this book has been compiled from a series of illustrated fact sheets published for the Rijksdienst voor de Monumentenzorg (Department for the Preservation of Monuments and Historic Buildings). The following people were among the contributors: *Towns and Villages:* F. W. van Voorden, L. Prins and M. E. Doets; *The House:* C. R. G. Hofstee; *Castles and Country Houses:* G. Roosegaarde Bisschop; *Churches:* W. F. Denslagen; *Farmhouses:* C. L. van Groningen and G. Berends; *Windmills:* G. H. Keunen and J. T. M. Gunneweg.
Compiler and editor-in-chief: A. P. Smaal.

Design: Peter Koch
ISBN: 90 246 4401 1
Dutch title: Kijken naar monumenten in Nederland

Translation: Ministry of Foreign Affairs, Translations Branch (J. S. Quysner)

Distribution for Belgium: Uitgeverij Westland, Schoten

Cover illustrations, top: Zuidhavenpoort bridge, Zierikzee; *centre* (from left to right): St. Stephen's Church, Nymegen, interior; Bovigne Castle, Ginneken; farmhouse at Bergambacht; *below:* hollow-post mill at Meerkerk.
Half-title page: Grote Kerk, Breda.
Title page: Oude Gracht, Utrecht (Jan de Beijer).
Page 4, top: carved lion at Bergh Castle, 's-Heerenberg; *below:* Culemborg Gate, Buren (Gelderland).
Page 5, top left: Doesburgermill, Ede; *top right:* miniature from a 15th-century book of hours; *centre:* farmhouse at Hoogwoud; *below left:* water-tower, Breda; *below right:* Verwerstraat, 's-Hertogenbosch.
Page 6: Weighhouse and cheese market, Alkmaar; detail from etching by Romeyn de Hooghe, 1674.

Contents

SPQA RESTITUIT VIRTUS ABLATÆ IURA BILANCIS

Preface

The Netherlands has a wealth of monuments and historic buildings, all of which add to the character and congeniality of its towns and villages. A country's architectural heritage says a lot about its history and culture. Dutch people are justly proud of their monuments and of the skill and craftsmanship which went into their design and construction. It is gratifying to know that there is also a great deal of interest abroad in Dutch monuments and how they are preserved and restored.

This book is the result of close collaboration between government and private conservation societies. I feel sure that it will stimulate international interest in the way we look after our monuments and I hope that it will encourage people to visit the Netherlands and see them for themselves.

Prince Claus
of the Netherlands

Towns and villages

Towns and villages as 'monuments'

The Netherlands is a small country with more than 14 million inhabitants and a growing need for housing and working accommodation.
New buildings are being put up and alterations to older properties are being carried out to meet present-day requirements and as a result, towns and villages are constantly changing. This process has of course been going on for centuries, but now it is more rapid and drastic than ever before. New building methods, the use of 'harder' building materials and the necessity to cater for traffic are some of the reasons behind this.

The historic buildings which have survived in our towns and villages have a special importance in our 20th-century urban environment.

However, despite the increase in interest in monuments and historic buildings in recent years, relatively little information is available about towns and villages as architectural 'monuments'.

Generally speaking, we do not know much about the development of towns and villages and the buildings in them. This chapter could therefore serve as an invitation to the reader to discover the history of towns and villages for himself, using the information it contains as a starting point.

Historic buildings are usually found in the centres of modern towns and villages, either in groups or singly. People were living and working in towns as early as the Middle Ages and consequently built houses, warehouses, public and military buildings and monasteries on sites which were important at the time. In and around the villages they built farms, castles and country houses.

The extent to which towns and villages have preserved their historic character depends on the changes to which they have been subjected. Much has been lost as a result of new roads, shops and office premises, and slum clearance, but where there has been little or no new development and the original layout of the streets and the old buildings has been retained, an area within a town or village can be regarded as being of historic and architectural interest.

There are still many of these areas all over the Netherlands, a large number of which are protected under the Monuments and Historic Buildings Act. For example, part of the centre of The Hague (right) is protected in this way, as is the small town of Buren in Gelderland (page 17) and the surrounding landscape. In the extreme south of Limburg, the hamlets of Plaat and Diependaal (page 10) and their scattered buildings are protected village landscapes.

View of Buren, drawing by J. de Beijer, De Pol Collection.

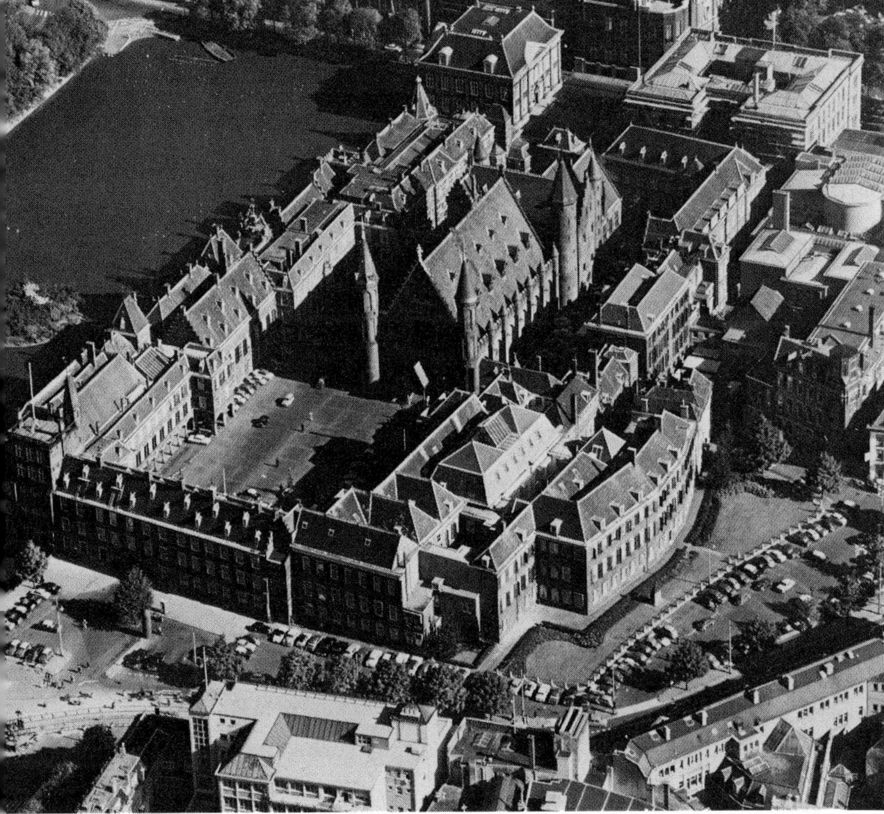

The Hague, Binnenhof and surroundings.

Plaat-Diependaal (Limburg).

The idea of conserving the historic centres of towns and villages as architectural monuments is not new, but it was revived in the late fifties as a reaction against post-war changes to the urban landscape. As a result of new housing and shopping requirements and of the need to make villages and town centres accessible, large-scale projects had been carried out with far-reaching consequences. Often buildings or whole streets which were of historic value had been demolished and then for various reasons the new buildings were not put up. Since 1961, the Monuments and Historic Buildings Act has made it possible to preserve whole areas of historic importance by means of careful renovation tailored to their historic character.

Our towns and villages as we know them today are the result of centuries of building grafted on to a basic structure. The main elements have scarcely changed. Key factors such as the nature of the terrain, the layout of the streets and the division of land into parcels remain constant. If anything has changed then it will be that the population has grown, causing settlements to expand outwards.

In theory it should be possible to make improvements while retaining the existing street layout and any buildings of value. The history of our towns is in fact the best proof that this can also be done in practice.

The origins of towns and villages

In comparison with its neighbours, the Netherlands is essentially a country of towns, most of which came into being between 1200 and 1400. There were no real cities except for Amsterdam, which in 1700 shared with London, Paris and Naples the distinction of being one of the four cities in Europe with more than 200,000 inhabitants.

The difference between a town and a village is difficult to define. A place used to be called a village if it had fewer than 1,500 inhabitants. If it had more and the life of the community no longer revolved round one activity – usually agriculture – it could, in theory, become a town and claim town rights. Towns are less easily defined in terms of size. Some were in fact no bigger than villages, while others had more than 20,000 inhabitants. They were usually the scene of many different activities and pursuits – trade, transport, crafts and administration – which could be seen in the different types of buildings. In addition to housing, a town had a town hall, a weighhouse, warehouses, churches and monasteries; for defence purposes there were military buildings and it was surrounded by fortifications.

No two towns are alike, either in terms of historical development or character. Villages possess features which are more characteristic of their region, such as layout (e.g. the villages in Drenthe built round a village green), farmhouse styles and the materials, such as roof thatching.

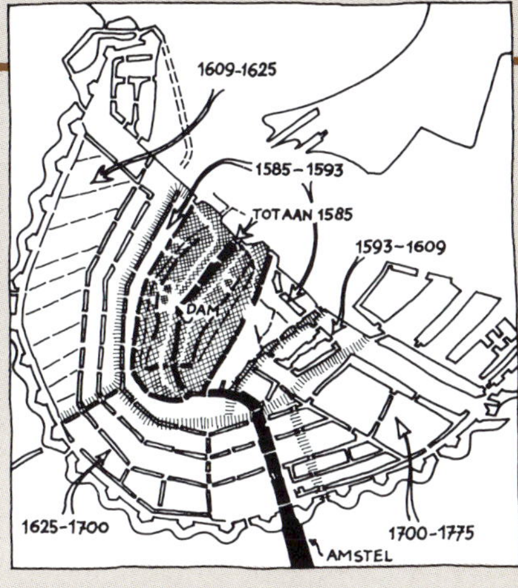

Amsterdam, which grew up around the Amstel dam. Successive additions are indicated on the map, which shows the city as it was in 1825.

Amsterdam, aerial photograph.

Villages

Dutch villages can be categorised according to their structural similarities. The 'terp' or *mound village* is characteristic of the low-lying regions of the Netherlands and clearly bears witness to the age-old struggle to repel the water. The houses and farms are constructed relativily close together on a man-made mound, or terp, in many cases clustered round the church and churchyard. Terp villages are to be found in a wide area along the coast of Groningen and Friesland.
The 'kerkringdorp' (ring-round-the-church village) found in Zeeland in some respects resembles the terp village. Here too the buildings are grouped around the church or churchyard but in this case they are situated on a natural elevation.
A completely different type the 'brinkdorp' (village round a green) is built around an open area or village green. A number of variations on this theme are found in the higher-lying sandy areas, notably in Drenthe where in contrast to other regions, the moisture level of the ground was not high. The buildings could be arranged more freely around the green since it was not necessary to take communal measures against the water. This type is also to be found in the sandy areas of Brabant, where the central open space is called the 'plaatse' and is frequently triangular.

Vlist (South Holland); ribbon development.

Marrum (Friesland), 'terpdorp' – village on man-made mound.

By contrast, some Dutch villages were built more or less in a straight line by the side of a road, dike, canal or river as a form of *ribbon development*. Such villages may consist of one or more lines or have houses along one side of the road or both. In the western part of the Netherlands ribbon development is common in marshy areas, where the starting point for the reclamation of the marshland was a river (such as the Vlist) or a road (as at Oud-Loosdrecht).
Ribbon development along dikes is to be found along the major rivers and on the coast of the IJsselmeer (what used to be Zuyder Zee). In the village of Durgerdam (page 14) the houses stand in a row along the dike which is the only habitable spot. Another kind of 'ribbon village' is situated in the older polders, where the roads were laid out according to a strict plan and served as a basis for the structure of the village. Middenbeemster is an example of this; it is built along two completely straight roads which intersect at right angles. Finally, ribbon development took place in the nineteenth century in the high fenlands of Groningen and Drenthe along canals depending on the drainage system.

Towns

Towns need to be viewed somewhat differently, since they, more than villages have been influenced by all kinds of variable factors. Moreover, most Dutch towns developed during the Middle Ages from older settlements, often of the village type, which means that each has acquired its own separate identity. A good example of this is Willemstad, which did not become a town until after the Middle Ages.

Middenbeemster (North Holland), village at the intersection of two roads.

Below: Elp (Drenthe), 'brinkdorp' – village around a green.

early 17th centuries the ports were greatly enlarged and equipped with new fortifications.
The second phase began with the Industrial Revolution in the nineteenth century. New economic developments and population growth – at first mainly in the large towns – led to the expansion of the towns. During the same period fortifications were dismantled, resulting in drastic changes to the appearance of the towns. In places where there was little need for building land, the sites of the fortifications were converted into

Durgerdam (North Holland), wooden houses on the dike.

It started like many villages in the sea-clay region of South-Holland and Zeeland as a group of houses clustered in a square round the church, with the main street on a straight axis leading to the dike. At the end of the sixteenth century the village was fortified, and ramparts and moats were constructed. The old village expanded within these fortifications by the addition of a number of parallel streets so that the town as it stands today consists of a number of different structural and architectural components.

Nevertheless a few general statements about the development of Dutch towns as a whole can be made. Two phases can be distinguished in their development and expansion: their beginnings and modest growth during the Middle Ages and second the period of expansion in the mid-nineteenth century. In practically the entire country, urban development was at a standstill from 1550 till 1850. The most important changes during this period took place on the outskirts of towns where extensive earthworks and moats were constructed outside the mediaeval walls.
In the sixteenth and seventeenth centuries under the Republic of the United Provinces, the main towns fortified in this manner were on the boundaries of Holland, the most important province, such as Den Briel, Heusden and Weesp, and those in strategic positions on the borders of the republic, such as Bergen op Zoom, Maastricht and Nymegen.
It was only in western Holland that the towns continued to expand between 1550 and 1750. In the late 16th and

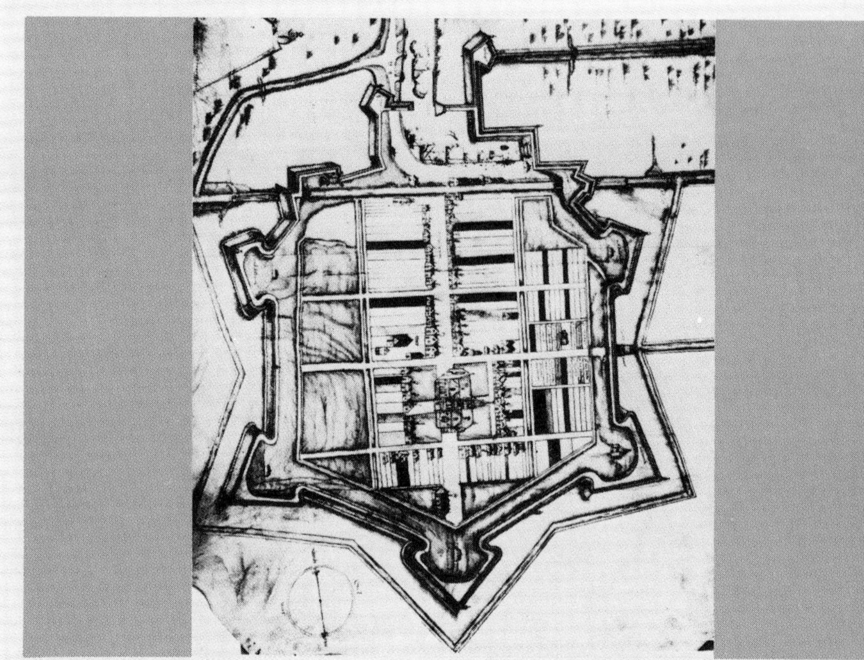

parks for the general public (examples are in Kampen and Zaltbommel).
A few towns – Gorinchem and Naarden for example – continued to play a military role and therefore retained their fortifications intact.
Another factor which influenced the historic layout of both towns and villages was the nature of the terrain.
Moreover, towns nearly always appeared at key points in the countryside, at points where roads and waterways converged, at the boundaries between high and low-lying land, and at the mouths of rivers.

Schoonebeek (Drenthe).

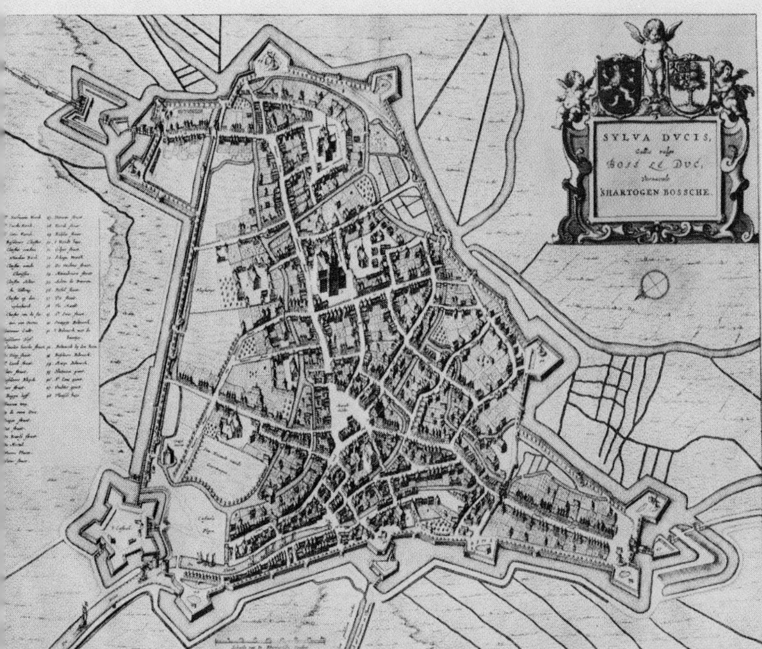

Above left: Willemstad (North Brabant), map from the 16th century.

Above left: Den Bosch, 17th century map.

Above right: Den Bosch, market place formed by the meeting of three roads.

Left: Willemstad (North Brabant).

Left: Elburg (Gelderland), rectangular layout.

Kampen (Overijssel); the gateway in the photograph is indicated by the arrow in the plan on the left.

Urban layout was also affected by features which were already there when the town came into being, such as through-roads, dikes and ditches, which were often incorporated into the new town. For example, one can still clearly see from the layout of Den Bosch that the three country roads which form a junction at the market place are the three oldest streets in the town. In Delft the sections into which the polders were divided are still apparent in the layout of the town, and the canals follow the course of former drainage ditches. A castle was another feature which influenced the formation of the town because the protection it afforded stimulated trade and industry. Most castles in towns are on the outskirts. In some towns as Culemborg and Buren, they disappeared after the Middle Ages, but their sites remain and can easily be identified even today. Once a town has taken shape its character is principally determined by the economic activities it fosters. The features of a port are different from those of a market town or industrial town; the transit of goods necessitated the building of warehouses, while an ecclesiastical centre such as Utrecht contains a relatively large number of churches and monasteries.

The influence of economic activities on the layout of towns can be seen from the fact that practically every town has a market place – then, as now, the centre of local trade. The influence of international trade, which was principally conducted along the main rivers and coastal waters, is reflected in inland and coastal ports. Shipping on the IJssel is specifically reflected in the plan of Kampen where about twelve streets lead to the water's edge. This dense network of streets leading to the river is a result of the close relationship between the town's economy and waterways.

The gradual and independent development of towns produced irregular layouts in which many older elements were preserved. There are very few towns in the Netherlands which were built in a relatively short period according to a plan: Elburg and Coevorden are exceptions.

The first expansion of the large towns occurred during the 19th century. Boulevards ('singels') were built on or near sites where fortifications had been demolished, and together with existing thoroughfares, these led to the construction of completely new districts. In towns like Utrecht and Maastricht the nineteenth-century buildings on the boulevards made a stately addition to the mediaeval town. In the big cities – Amsterdam, The Hague and Rotterdam – separate districts sprang up outside the old centres.

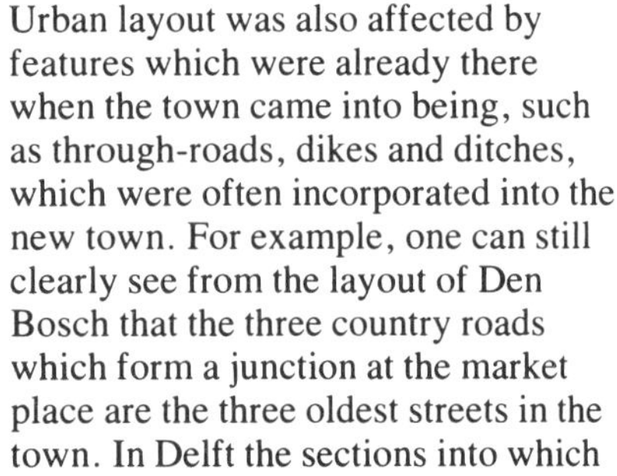

Delft, layout of streets based on polder drainage ditches, aerial photograph 1920.

Protecting our towns and villages is not just a question of preserving historic architecture in its setting but of conserving settlements as they have developed through the ages. Old maps can teach us a lot about the development of towns and villages. Those of Jacob van Deventer (below), a geographer in the service of King Philip II of Spain, are more or less the oldest surviving series of maps of Dutch towns. Though drawn up between 1555 and 1572 they give us a fairly accurate picture of the late mediaeval town, as the fortifications they depict are primarily mediaeval. The buildings are grouped together, except for the public ones – the town

Delft, the Oude Delft.

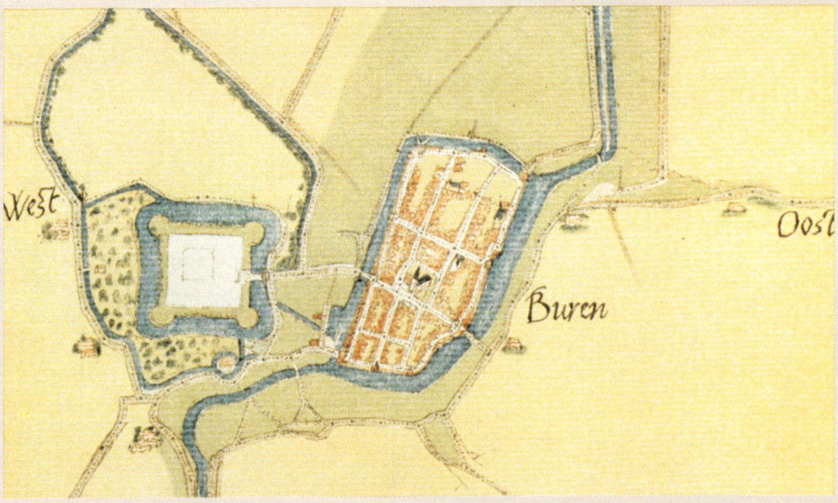

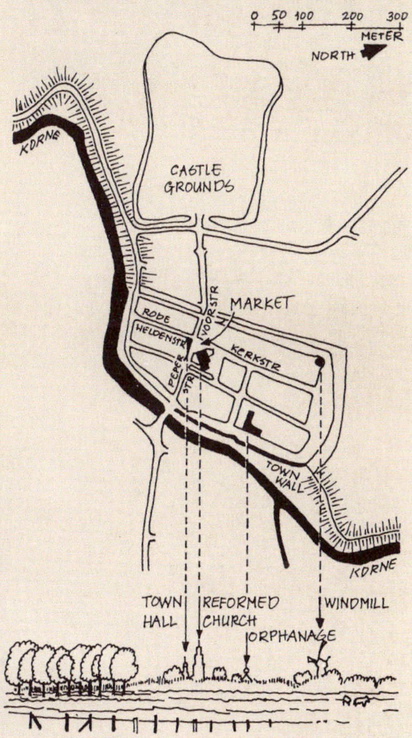

Above left: Buren (Gelderland), map by Jacob van Deventer, circa 1560.

Buren (Gelderland).

Buren (Gelderland), town wall along the river Korne with the orphanage in the background.

gates, churches and monasteries – which are indicated individually. More detailed maps and bird's eye views from the 16th and 17th centuries (Braun-Hogeberg, Guicciardini and Johan Blaeu), not all of which are as reliable, give an idea of the appearance of the larger towns.

In the case of the fortified towns they give a clear picture of the layout of the fortifications at the time of the war of liberation against Spain (1568-1648) and later. By comparing these old maps with recent ones and with aerial photographs, it is fairly easy to ascertain which elements have changed.

Buren (Gelderland), Rodeheldenstraat.

Buren, an example of a protected townscape

We have chosen Buren as an example of a protected townscape where the historic features are clearly recognisable within a relatively small area. This little town is more or less rectangular, with a wall on the south and west sides along the Korne, a tributary of the Linge, and with a late fourteenth-century moat on the north and west sides. The castle (which is no longer standing) clearly influenced the town's development.

The earliest buildings must have stood along the river wall. The town proper began to develop after the foundation of a chapel by Alard van Buren between 1367 and 1395 on the site of the present Dutch Reformed Church. This formed the centre of what later evolved into the town – the market place, a fairly small triangular space at the junction of the two main streets (Voorstraat-Peperstraat and Rodeheldenstraat-Kerkstraat). The Culemborg gate stands at the west end of the Voorstraat. The town centre is enclosed by a row of houses built into the wall on either side of the Culemborg gate. The sixteenth-century town hall stands on the corner of Peperstraat and Rodeheldenstraat; alterations were made to it in 1608 and 1739-40 and it has recently been restored. The Weighhouse, an early nineteenth-century wooden colonade, is built against the façade of the church beside the town pump dating from 1732. The more compact 'urban' built-up area has remained restricted to the south of the town, while to the north, the gardens and orchards of the town farms which had always occupied a large proportion of the area within the walls, have been replaced by housing in the last few decades. A fine historic monument in this part of

Buren (Gelderland), Rodeheldenstraat, drawing of façades in the development plan.

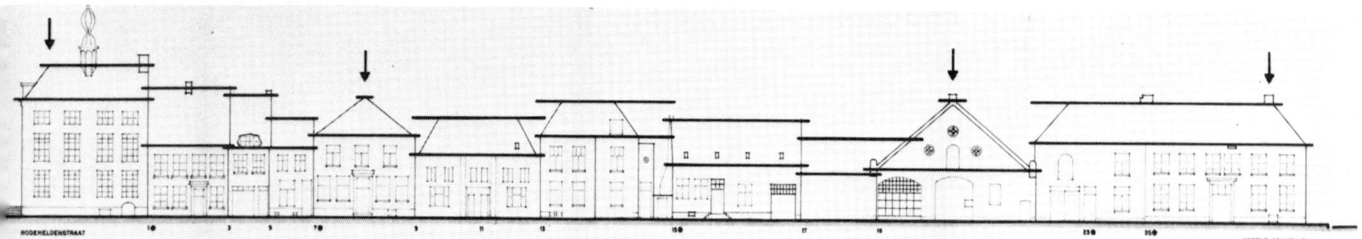

Delft, market place.

the town is the orphanage founded in 1612 by Maria Countess of Nassau on the site of a Franciscan monastery dating from 1420. The northwest corner of the town wall is accentuated by the 'Prince of Orange' windmill. On the west side of the town is the site of the former castle. To the north and northwest there is extensive meadowland. To the south and east, between the wall and the Korne, there is a stretch of land which, for centuries, has been used for allotments. The ground between the south bank of the Korne and the 'Erichemsekade' serves as kitchen gardens and orchards and forms a charming contrast to the town rising above it.

Sittard (Limburg), market place.

Delft market place/Sittard market place

There are similarities between the houses in Delft and Sittard – the living accommodation above shops and cafés, the T-shaped nineteenth century windows, the alternation of brick and plaster façades – but there are also differences. The most striking ones are in the roofs and in the width of the façades. These particular features are essential aspects of the character of a town and distinguish the houses in Sittard and Maastricht, both in South Limburg, from those in the rest of the Netherlands.

Houses in all the Dutch provinces, except Limburg, usually have the roof ridge running at right angles to the façade and thus to the street.

The height and breadth of the houses and their roofs determine the character of a town. In the narrow streets the top of the façade (gable or cornice) is of particular importance. The gradual transition from gables (including stepped gables) to cornices therefore

Schoonhoven (South Holland), Haven 82; the different phases are clearly recognizable.

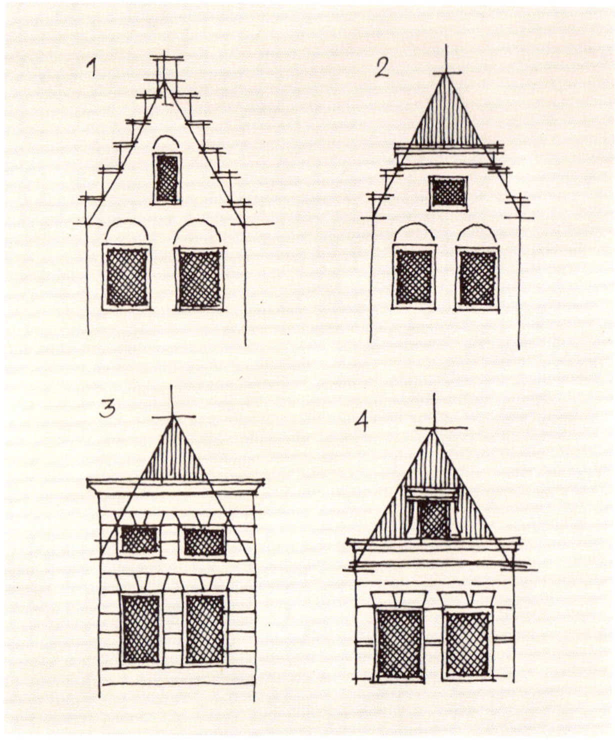

Possible alterations of gables from stepped gable 1 to types 2, 3 or 4.

affected these streets considerably. In the eighteenth and nineteenth centuries many sixteenth and seventeenth-century gables were converted into cornices for constructional reasons, but also as a sign of prosperity. At the same time the crossbar windows were replaced by sash windows and the façade was plastered. Only in a few cases were houses rebuilt from scratch. The basic design of the town houses frequently dates from the sixteenth or seventeenth century.

The successive alterations which have been made at No. 69 on Delft market place (see page 19) are quite obvious. As it originally stood in 1657 (the year is shown on the façade), the house had a gable which was later replaced by a cornice. In the nineteenth century the house was plastered and T-shaped windows, now spoiled, were put in. The double door, permitting double occupancy, also dates from the nineteenth century. Despite all these changes, the basic harmony of the design of the façade has been retained and the nineteenth century exterior makes a positive contribution to the historic character of the town.
When changes are made without consideration for their architectural effect the result is façades of the kind shown in the Schoonhoven example; since only the most essential elements have been modernised, much of the original design of the façade has survived.

Gouda, Wijdstraat, looking west from St. John's Church.

Geertruidenberg (North Brabant), market place.

Zierikzee (Zeeland).

The house

Throughout the Netherlands there are towns or villages where the style and intimacy of the old buildings have a charm which immediately makes us feel at home. Such places have a special atmosphere which allows us to appreciate their historic architecture in peace, an atmosphere which it is not easy to describe but which nonetheless can readily be experienced.

The Netherlands is particularly fortunate in having a rich heritage of historic buildings. Every day Dutch people pass churches, town halls, farmhouses, castles, windmills and houses which are monuments to the lifestyle of their fore-fathers. In some cases the irreplaceable value of old buildings has only been realised after they have been demolished, when it has become apparent just how important they are to us.

We all need to feel at home in our surroundings, and historic buildings and monuments help to create a sense of identity as well as providing a pleasing environment in which to live and work.

They contribute to our well-being by telling us about the history and culture of our fore-fathers. For all of these reasons it makes sense to protect them from demolition.

Houses deserve special consideration amongst the various categories of historic buildings. They provide us with insight into economic and social conditions in former times and show how man has built his home both to suit his needs and according to the contents of his pocket.

Originally streets were the focal point of the life of the community; they were places where people met and conducted their business. Nowadays, many of them have had their original function restored as pedestrian precincts, and these traffic-free streets make it much easier to 'read' about the history of a place in the buildings themselves.

This chapter contains a brief guide to historic Dutch houses and emphasizes the importance of protecting historic buildings.

The Oudegracht in Utrecht, drawing by Jan van Goyen, approx. 1650; Boymans-van Beuningen Museum, Rotterdam.

'The Little Street', painting by Johannes Vermeer; Rijksmuseum, Amsterdam.

Maastricht, Stenenbrug 12.

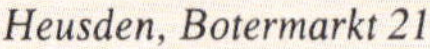

Heusden, Botermarkt 21.

Voorburg, Herenstraat 4.

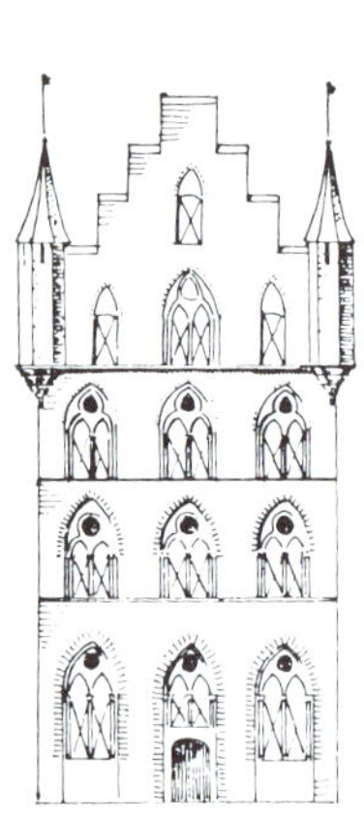

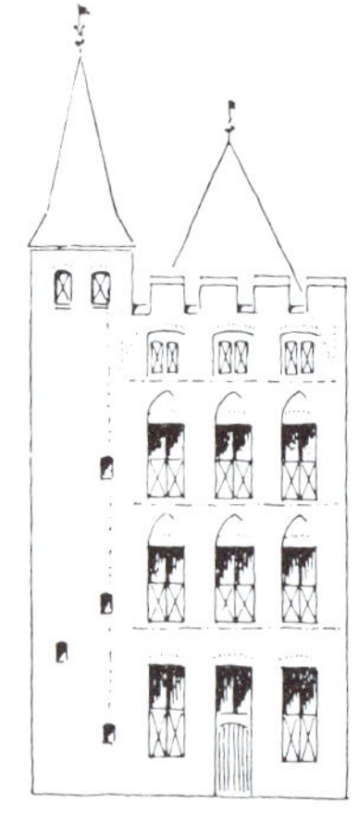

Right: Wooden façade of house in the gardens of the Zeeland Museum, Middelburg.

Far left: Reconstruction of the façade, with turrets, of the Fresenburch house, Oude Gracht 113, Utrecht.

Left: Reconstruction of the façade of the Oudaen house, Oudegracht 99, Utrecht.

During his travels in 1650 and 1651, Jan van Goyen made a drawing of the Oudegracht canal in Utrecht (page 23). Although the sketch dates from the 17th century, it gives a pretty good picture of how the towns must have looked three centuries earlier, with the stone houses of the nobility towering above the small wooden houses of the ordinary townsfolk.

The Fresenburch house (above left), built in the 13th century, has battlements along the side walls and turrets at the corners of its façade. The Oudaen house (above right), which was built in the early 14th century, has a wall-walk with battlements, a covered parapet and an impressive stair tower in one corner. Wall walks, battlements and turrets are features derived from castles in the country and give the earliest stone townhouses a powerful and dominant appearance.

Trefoil arch.

Oosterhout, St. Janstraat 22.

Gouda, Catharina Hospital.

Dordrecht, Hofstraat 8.

Fortified houses, however, did not play any major part in defending towns protected by walls. This can be seen from the fact that the doors and windows open directly on to the street. However, when citizens were involved in a dispute with one another the rival factions bombarded their opponents from their homes. The original walls were a metre or more thick to make sure that construction was sound. These heavy, high, continuous walls also provided protection against fire; the corridor of the wall walk channelled off rain-water.

At first the houses of ordinary citizens resembled farmhouses. However, as merchants and artisans began to form an increasingly large section of the urban population, the wooden houses began to change, partly because the requirements of their inhabitants differed from those of the farmer and partly because there was no room for a yard around houses in the city. They were in fact built practically on top of each other. Wooden town houses began to acquire their own distinctive features: they became taller and usually had no side-windows.

Both fortified and wooden houses disappeared almost entirely in the course of the 15th and 16th centuries, merging as it were into one type.

A mediaeval city packed with thatched, wooden houses was a serious fire risk and many a town went up in flames on more than one occasion. In an effort to prevent this, the municipal authorities encouraged or compelled citizens to construct stone houses covered with roofing tiles or slates. However, stone houses with wooden façades – with the big advantage of many windows – were permitted in some cities until the 17th century.

A 19th century drawing depicts a

Right: Wooden house, Verwerstraat, 's-Hertogenbosch.

Far right: Detail from 'The Disbanding of the Provincial Militia at Utrecht', painting by Pauwels van Hillegaert, 1627; Rijksmuseum, Amsterdam.

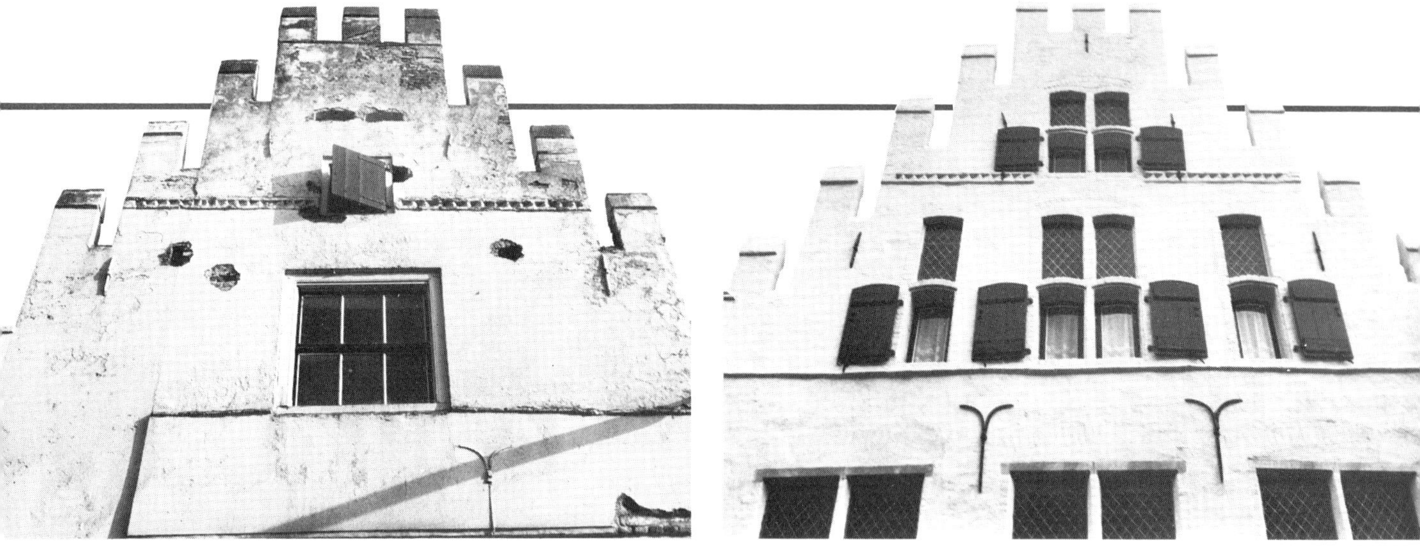

Upper façade prior to renovation, in 1970. Donkerstraat 26, Harderwijk.

Façade after renovation.

wooden façade in the Verwerstraat in 's-Hertogenbosch (page 25) which has since been demolished. In order to reduce rain damage, the façade inclined forwards slightly and each storey stuck out above the one below. The stone façades often sloped forwards. The shutters on these houses were made to open upwards and downwards; the lower shutters were used to display merchandise, while the upper ones protected the goods from the sun or the rain. Because there were originally no panes behind the shutters, life inside the house and outside on the street mingled much more than they do nowadays.

A house with a wooden façade in Middelburg (page 24) dating from the early 16th century survived into the second half of the 19th century but was unfortunately demolished in 1888. A hundred years ago there was little interest in the interiors of such simple dwellings but the façade was saved and transported to the gardens of the Zeeland Museum. The shutters open to the side; originally the lower half of the windows on the first floor and the attic had shutters only and no glass. The upper part of the façade is decorated with a trefoil arch.

Fortified townhouses were not easy to defend, but they did not need to be in a walled town. However, high gables, battlements and turrets were added to houses as symbols of power and strength; sometimes, to further this impression, the façade was built up higher than the roof behind it. Such a 'sham gable' with battlements can be seen in a detail from 'The Disbanding of The Provincial Militia at Utrecht' by Pauwels van Hillegaert (page 25).

Later, most stone houses were built with pointed gables just like the wooden houses before them, and they also had an inner frame made entirely or partly of wood. The wooden framework supporting the weight of the building enabled the stone walls to be thinner, thus making a stone house less expensive.

The Templars' house in Zierikzee (left) is an early 15th century example

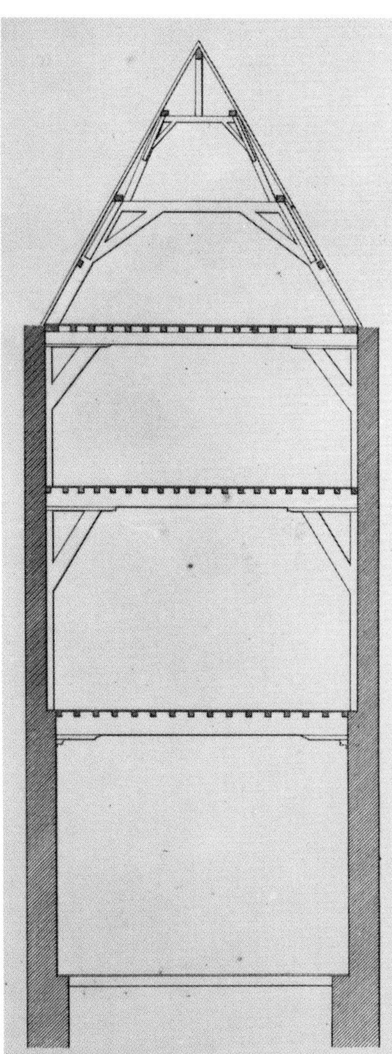

Drawing made in 1888 of the Templars' house, Meelstraat 1, Zierikzee.

Weighhouse and cheese market, Alkmaar; etching by Romeyn de Hooghe, 1674, Teylers Museum, Haarlem.

Aerial photograph of the market place in Alkmaar, 1952.

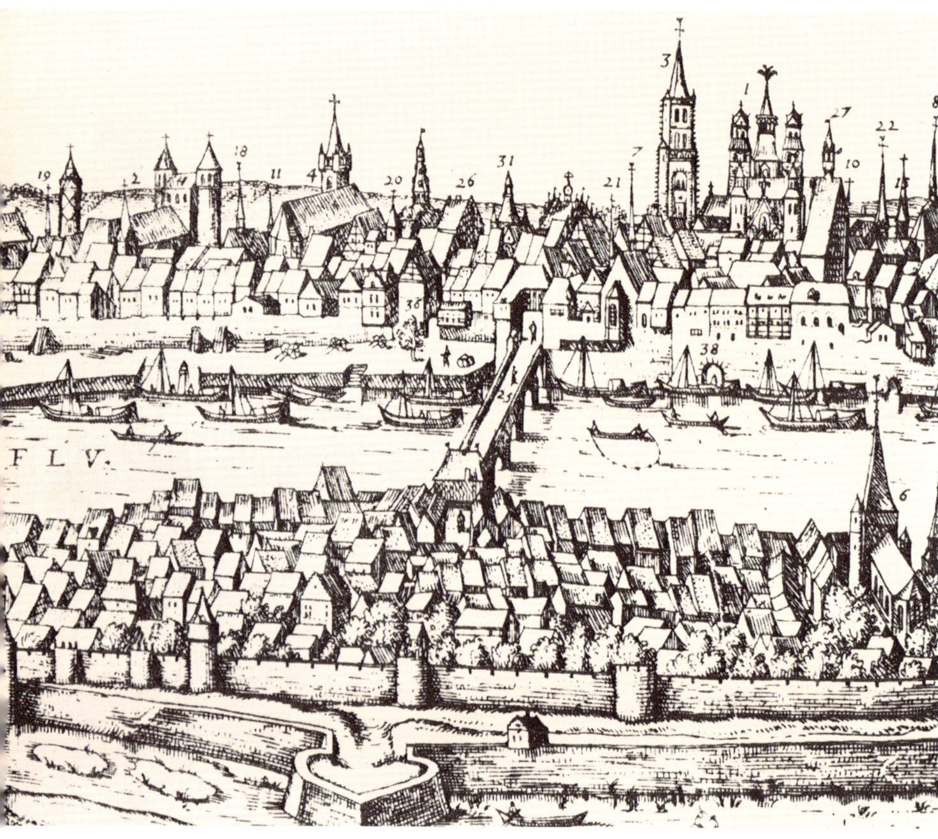

View of Maastricht, etching from a drawing by Simon de Bellomonte, approx. 1575.

of such a house. The ground floor beams are supported by the wall, the upper floors have a wooden framework keeping the whole together. The front gable is constructed from brick and natural stone. The windows are placed in recesses, which prevent rain from getting in while accentuating the vertical lines of the building. The pointed arcs on the ground floor and in the gable are decorated with a trefoil pattern.

The stepped gable of a late 15th century house in Harderwijk (page 26) resembles the battlements of fortified houses, but the deep indentations reveal that the gable towers above the roof. There are four windows in the shape of a cross in the middle of the gable with fixed lights on either side. The leaded lights are slightly recessed to prevent rain from getting in. Originally the lower halves of the windows had shutters only. A rabbet was made in the brickwork to hold the shutters which could thus close tightly. A comparison of the gable before and after restoration reveals what can be hidden behind a thick layer of plaster.

The increasing use of brick and stone for building purposes in towns in the 15th and 16th centuries meant that street plans and the ground taken up by buildings were fixed and have remained the same until the present day. One thing which greatly influences the overall impression created by a town is the orientation of the ridges of the roofs. A 1674 painting by Romeyn de Hooghe (page 27) shows that the ridges of all the houses round the market place in Alkmaar were at right angles to the street. Although the houses to the right of the weighhouse were demolished about 1680 to allow the market place to be enlarged, the character of the area has remained the same, as can be seen from the aerial photograph (page 27).

A drawing by Simon de Bellomonte (above) dating from approx. 1575, shows that Maastricht was entirely different, as the ridges ran parallel to the street. This style of building is still found in Maastricht and many other places in the south and east.

The façades of shops and merchants' houses retained a wooden lower section until well into the 17th century. These sections contained numerous windows to allow plenty of light to fall on the interior. The street side of the ground floor usually served as a workshop, shop or office, while the back of the house was used as living quarters. The cross-section and the three-dimensional sketch show that this type of house often had an entresol above the living room behind the high-ceilinged front room. In winter this considerably reduced heat loss in the living room where there was usually a fire, whilst the chimney helped to warm the entresol which was often a bedroom. The cellar usually served as a kitchen but was sometimes let as a store-room, workshop or as living quarters. The rooms of the upper storeys were reserved for domestic purposes like storing, mangling and drying clothes, or storing peat and logs. In the 18th century people also began to live in these rooms.

View of the Stokstraat district of Maastricht from the river Maas.

Leidsegracht 2, 4 and 6 and Herengracht 394 after the fire in 1684; etching from the 'Brandenboek' (Book of Fires) by Jan van der Heiden

Leidsegracht 2, 4 and 6, Amsterdam.

Prins Hendrikkade 135, 136 and 137, Amsterdam.

Three houses in the Leidsegracht in Amsterdam (page 29) are a good example of such houses; each has retained some of the original features characteristic of the period around 1680. Number 6, on the left, has retained the heavy, wooden beam supporting the upper storeys in the otherwise 19th century façade. The outside steps have been removed and the main entrance has been moved to the basement, as frequently happened in the 19th century. Number 4 has a low entresol where the leaded lights used to be. The fact that the centre window on the third floor is lower than the others is an indication that it was originally a door to the storage room closed by shutters. Number 2 has partly retained the wooden beam in the façade.

There was a marked preference for

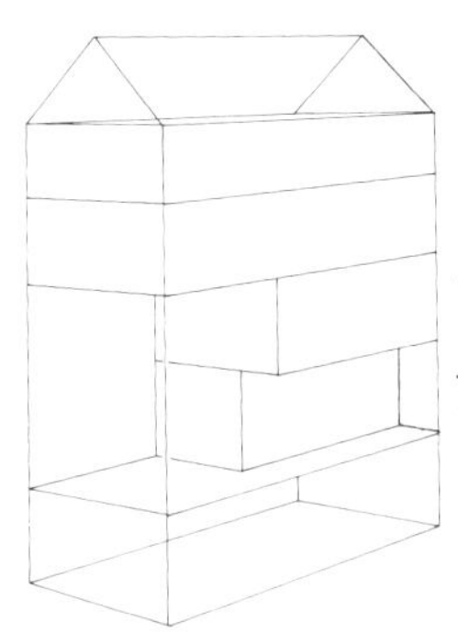

Three-dimensional sketch of a house with cellar, ground floor with entresol and two storeys.

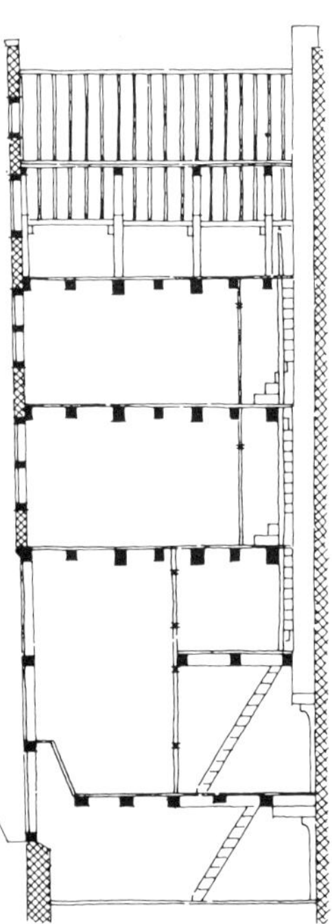

Cross-section of Olofspoort 7, Amsterdam; an example of a house with cellar, ground floor with entresol with upper room, two storeys and raised loft.

The Oudegracht in Utrecht, drawing by Jan de Beyer, 1753; Utrecht, municipal archives.

cornice gables towards the end of the 17th century and this lasted until well into the 19th century. New houses were built with such gables and older houses were adapted to suit the style of the day.
For example, the corner house on the Prins Hendrikkade in Amsterdam (page 30) was given an impressive cornice at the end of the 18th century. However, the lower wooden façade and the entresol betray the building's real age. The next house has a 19th century cornice, but the tackle and the small hip roof above the front part of the house indicate that it once had a shaped gable. The lower centre windows in the upper storeys of this and the neighbouring house reveal that there used to be shutters here.

Two houses in the Rotterdamsekaai in Middelburg (left) show how a shaped gable can be converted to a cornice gable more economically. At this time renovating a house often implied applying a white facing, made to resemble freestone.

The drawings by Jan de Beyer (1753) (below left) and R. Craayvanger (below) (about 1830) of the Oudegracht in Utrecht clearly show the extent to which the preference for the cornice gable changed the appearance of the town. They also show that all the windows have been altered and that all the shutters, signs, street stalls and benches have disappeared.
These 'modernized' façades therefore hide many features of much older architecture.

Rotterdamsekaai 1, Middelburg.

The Oudegracht, Utrecht; lithograph by R. Craayvanger, approx. 1830; Utrecht, municipal archives.

Groot Hertoginnelaan, The Hague.

Until the 19th century, the boundaries of a town or city were marked by walls beyond which it was not allowed to expand, but, after the Napoleonic period, the privileges enjoyed by towns disappeared. Ever since, the urban character of a community has been determined by its economic activities, the number of its inhabitants and the administrative and cultural infrastructure.
In the second half of the 19th century the fortifications in most towns were demolished, as they had not served any useful purpose for some time. Walls were often replaced by beautiful parks, along the edges of which wealthy citizens built elegant white-washed houses. The houses in the Stationstraat in Bergen op Zoom (below) which were built around 1870, are a good example of this.

Towards the end of the 19th century, whole new districts appeared around the centres of towns, often in neo-renaissance style. Architects between 1880 and 1900 were inspired by renaissance architecture and especially by Dutch examples of the 16th and 17th centuries. Designs were extremely sober as far as houses for the working-class were concerned, but very extravagant if the houses were for the wealthy, as can be seen in the Groot Hertoginnelaan in The Hague (above).

South side of Stationsstraat, Bergen op Zoom.

Urban expansion at the end of the 19th century was the result of the tremendous rural exodus by people who were drawn to the towns by commerce and industry. This resulted in old town centres becoming over-crowded and in atrocious housing conditions. The old districts where poorer people lived had not been built to accommodate such large numbers, and over-population and lack of maintenance reduced the houses to slums. This explains why in the towns very few small houses like the ones in the Oostdwarsgracht in Leiden (right) dating from about 1700 have survived to the present day.

Oostdwarsgracht 16 and 18, Leiden.

Enlightened industrialists who had the interest of their employees at heart made efforts to improve the housing conditions of their workers. For instance in 1882 the Yeast and Spirits Factory in Delft created the Agneta Park (below). The project took four years to complete and included houses for the employees, a villa for the director and numerous educational and recreational facilities.

The 1901 Housing Act brought about a general improvement. Housing associations were formed which received government subsidies to build decent houses for workers – usually smaller, simplified versions of the homes of the wealthy.
Some architects of the Amsterdam School, however, had a more individual style; in their eyes, a housing block was not a tower or a series of uniform dwellings but a total composition with a character of its own, independent of the style of the villas or residences of the rich.

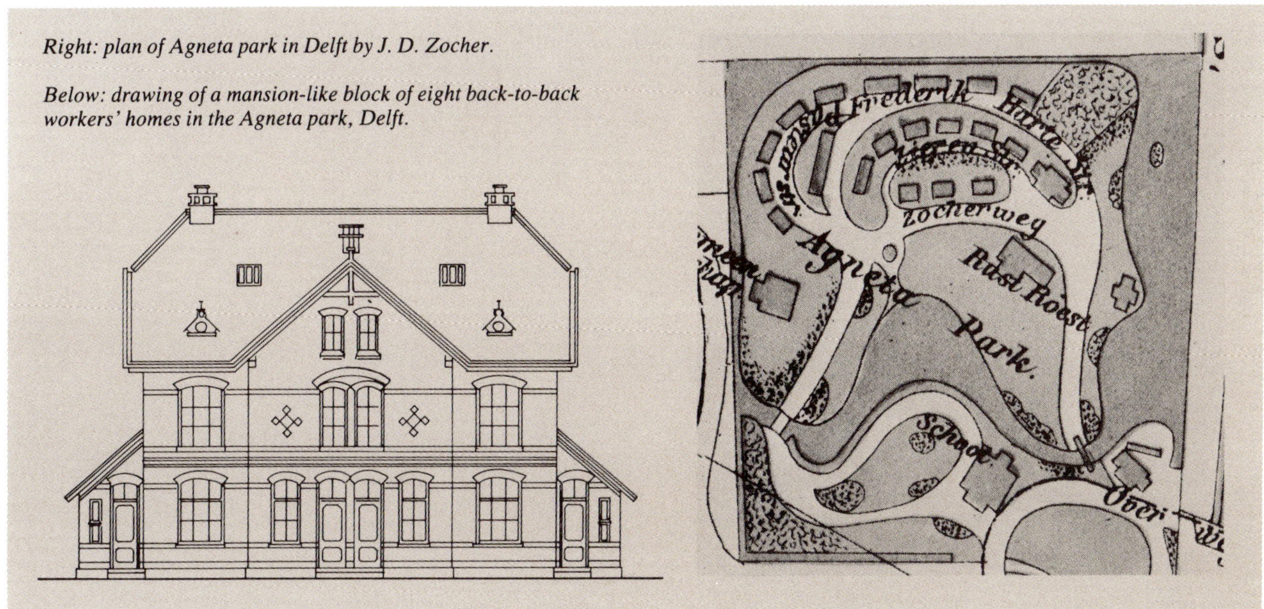

Right: plan of Agneta park in Delft by J. D. Zocher.

Below: drawing of a mansion-like block of eight back-to-back workers' homes in the Agneta park, Delft.

Side elevation of a plan for the Hembrugstraat, Amsterdam by M. de Klerk.

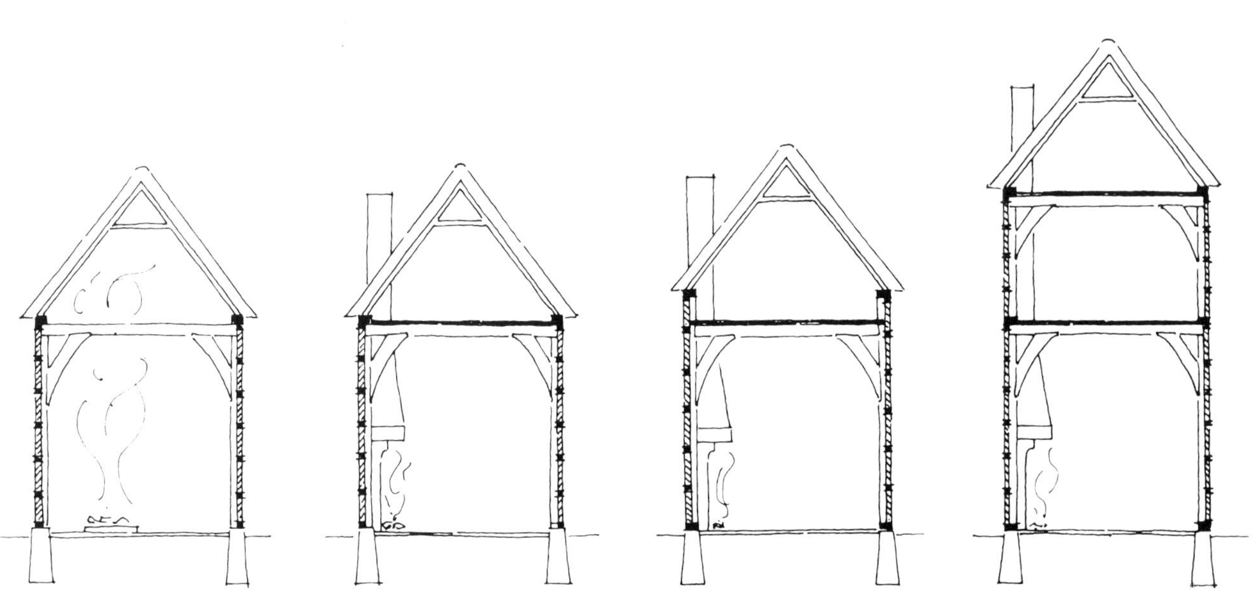

Wooden house with central fire.

Wooden house with stone chimney.

Wooden house with raised loft.

Wooden house with one storey.

The cross-sections (below) show the main phases in the development of the mediaeval townhouse.
The oldest type has an open fire on the ground floor; the smoke which collected under the thatched roof was led off through a hole.
In the 15th century most houses were furnished with a stone fireplace and flue against one wall which made it possible to construct a floored loft.
By lowering the loft floor slightly, the loft gained vertical walls, thus increasing the storage space considerably. It was a small step from this to the creation of another storey.

Although the chimneys were of stone, there was still a great fire risk owing to the thatched roofs and it was for this reason that in about 1500 most towns insisted that roofs should be covered with tiles or slates. This heavier type of 'hard' roofing, together with the weight of the loft floor, meant that solid stone foundations were essential. The space between the foundation walls could be used wholly or partly as a cellar.
To reduce the fire risk even more, thin stone walls instead of wooden ones were constructed around the wooden framework. They were secured to the framework by means of iron wall ties. In the 16th century these clamps were often decorated with beautiful wrought-iron work.

As the Netherlands has little natural stone, brick has played an important role in the history of Dutch architecture. The technique of brick-making, which was lost with the fall of the Roman Empire, was rediscovered in the 12th century. Bricks were very expensive at first, and so it was a long time before they were used for the houses of ordinary citizens.

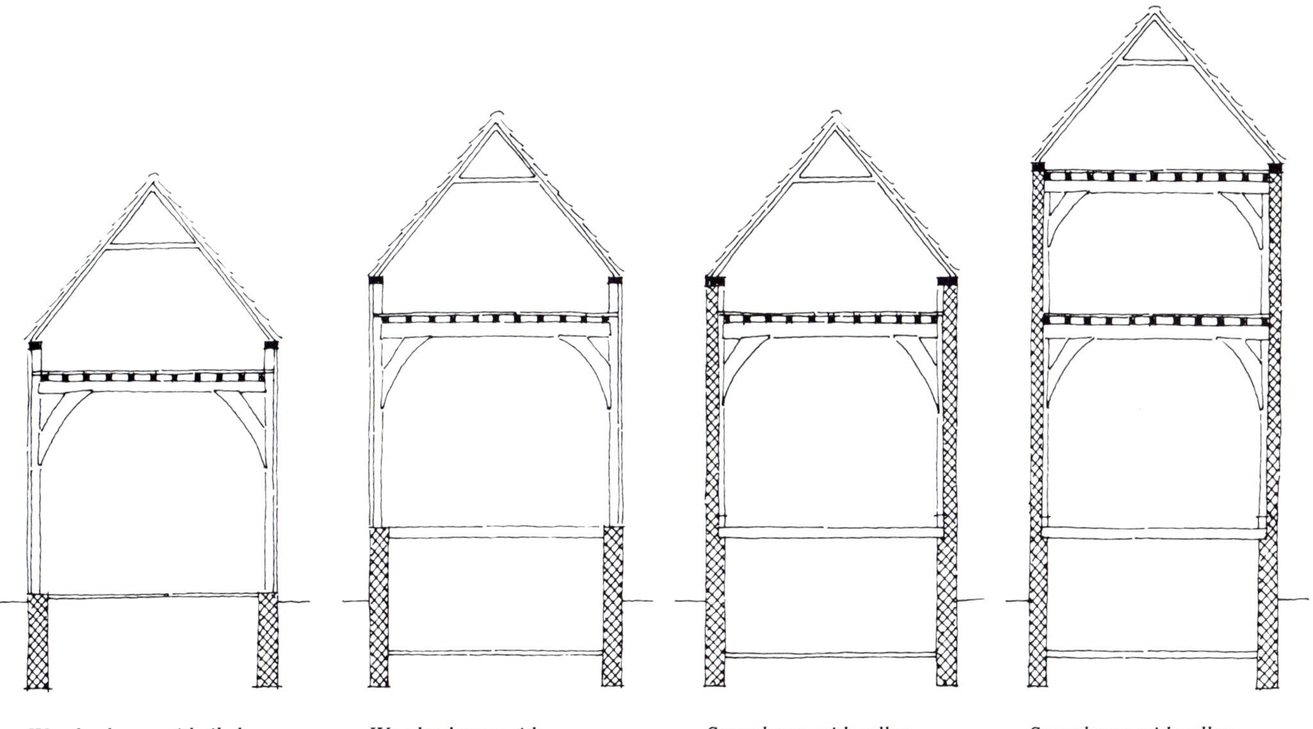

Wooden house with tiled roof and stone foundations.

Wooden house with cellar.

Stone house with cellar and raised loft.

Stone house with cellar and one storey.

The photographs show the main types of gable decoration, of which there are countless variations. The crow-step, straight, bottle-neck and bell gables are basically triangular; the first two are the earliest forms of gable decoration, the bottle-neck and bell gables appearing in the 17th and 18th centuries. The cornice gable was especially fashionable in the 18th and 19th centuries.

Straight gable

Crow-step gable

The five plans sketch the development of the Dutch house. The interior was gradually divided into more rooms and a hallway was incorporated about the middle of the 17th century. As Dutch houses are rather narrow on the whole, the entrance was moved from the centre to the corner of the façade, but broader houses retained a central entrance. The introduction of the hall and the stairs near the front door resulted in the segregation of life inside the house from life outside; friends, visitors and customers could no longer come and go as easily. At the end of the 17th century the staircase changed from a spiral staircase at the front to a staircase towards the back of the house.

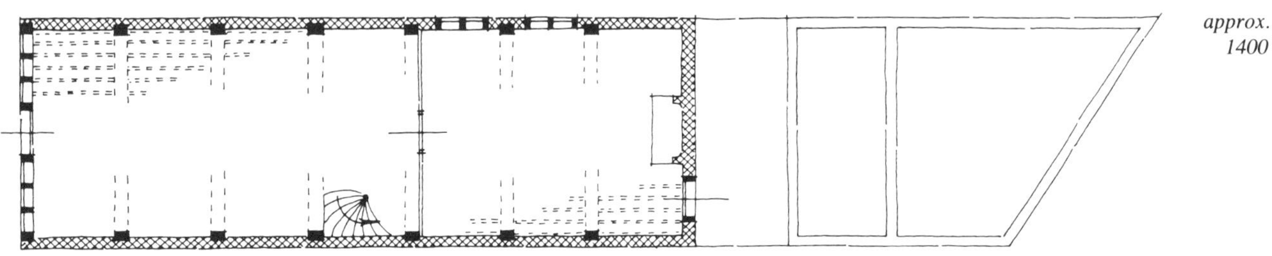

approx. 1400

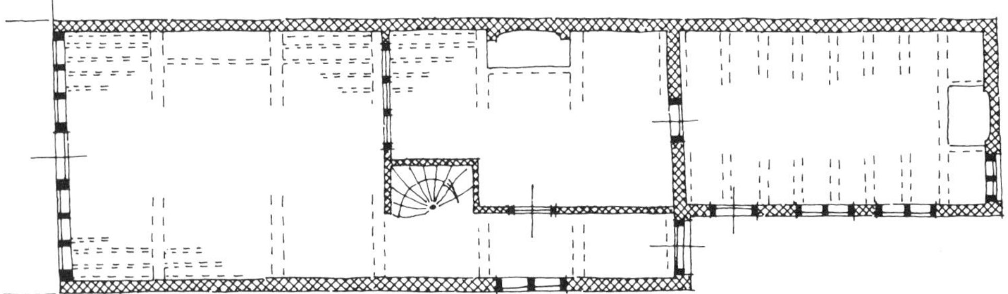

1612

Bottle-neck gable

Raised bottle-neck gable

Bell gable

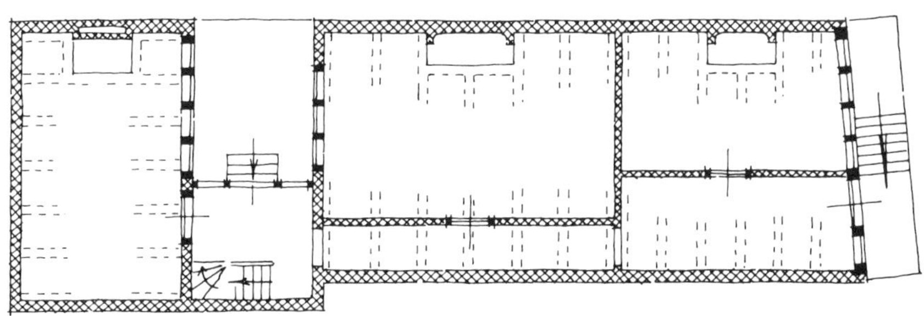

1660

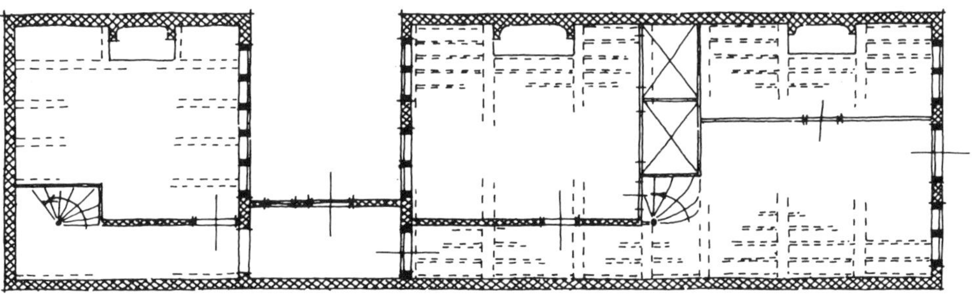

1659

1728

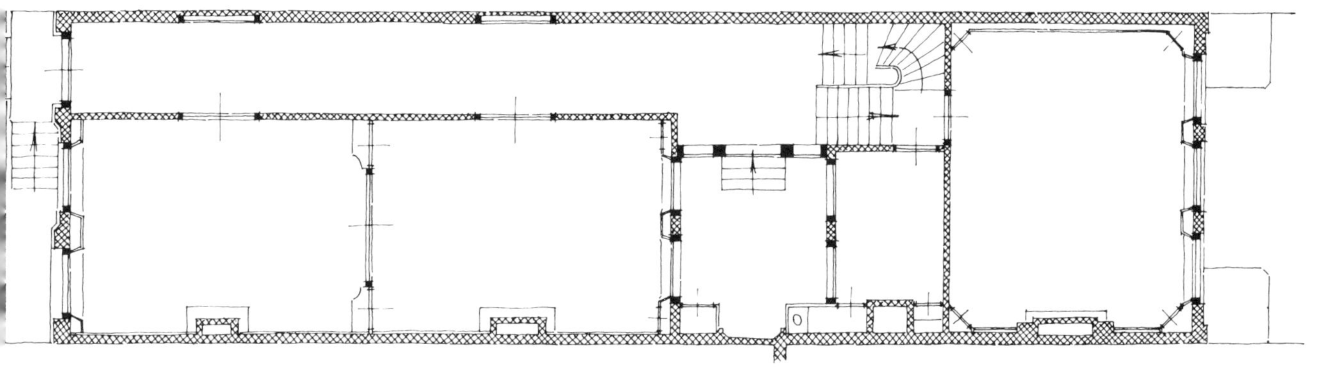

Cornice gable with crest

Cornice gable with balustrade

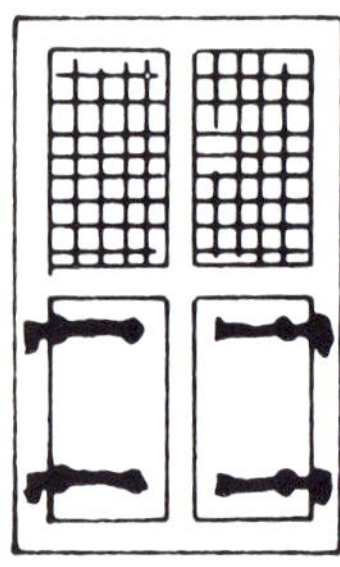

Window with leaded lights above and shutters below (16th and 17th century).

Window with rods in the upper frame and hinged windows with rods below (approx. 1650-1700).

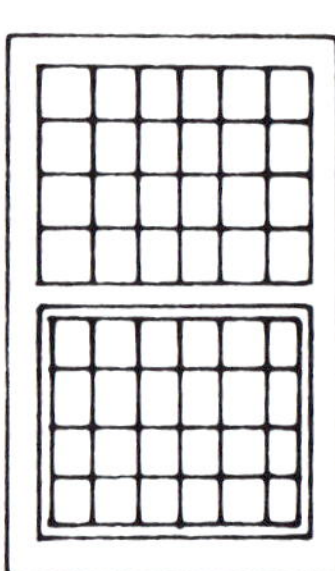

Window with rods in the upper frame and in the sliding section below (late 17th century – 18th century).

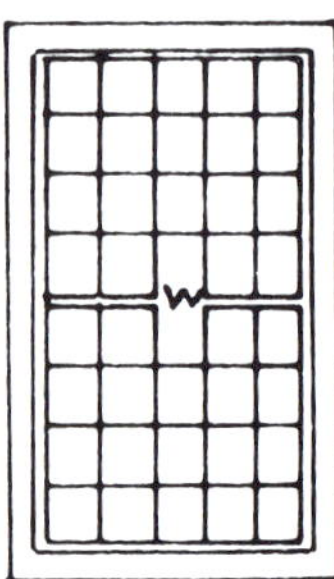

Double-hung window with sash fastener (late 17th century – 18th century).

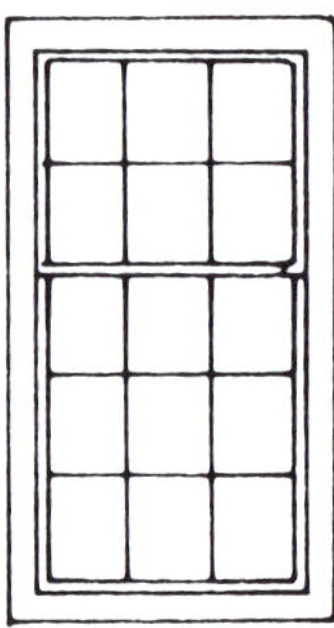

Sash window with sliding lower sash (late 18th century – 19th century).

Empire window; with hinged sashes below (late 18th century – 19th century).

Empire sash window; lower section slides (19th century).

T-window with sliding lower sash (late 19th, early 20th century).

Window with very large panes (20th century).

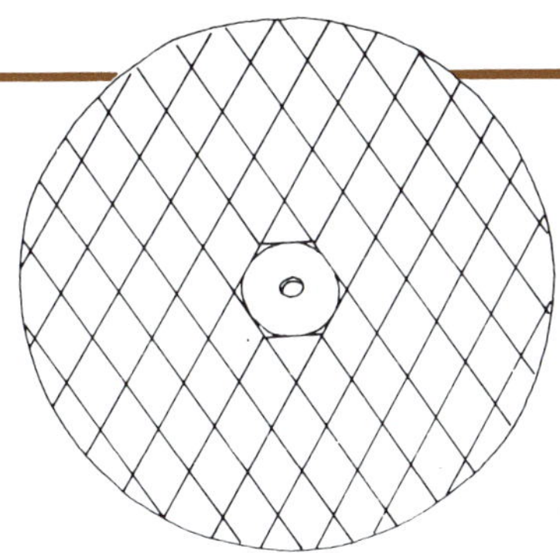

Glass disc divided into panes

Saddle roofs and hip roofs are the most common types of roof construction in the Netherlands. The mansard roof, which was introduced from France, was especially fashionable at the end of the 19th century and early 20th century. Roofs are usually covered with red or blue tiles. Slates are rare as they were too expensive.

Windows constitute an interesting feature of the house as they reveal a lot about its history. For a long time it was only possible to make glass discs; these were cut into panes which were held in place by lead strips. In the 16th century, small, rectangular panes were cut from plates of glass. As the quality of the glass improved, the panes became larger and were held in place by wooden rods rather than lead strips, which would not have provided enough support. The windows on the main floors of old houses were frequently modernized, with one large pane replacing numerous small ones in the original frame.

The fact that shutters were replaced by panes in the lower halves of the windows in the 17th century indicates that the window played an important role in the gradual separation of street life from life inside the home, the shop or the work-shop. It was no longer necessary to have contact with the street in order to let in light.

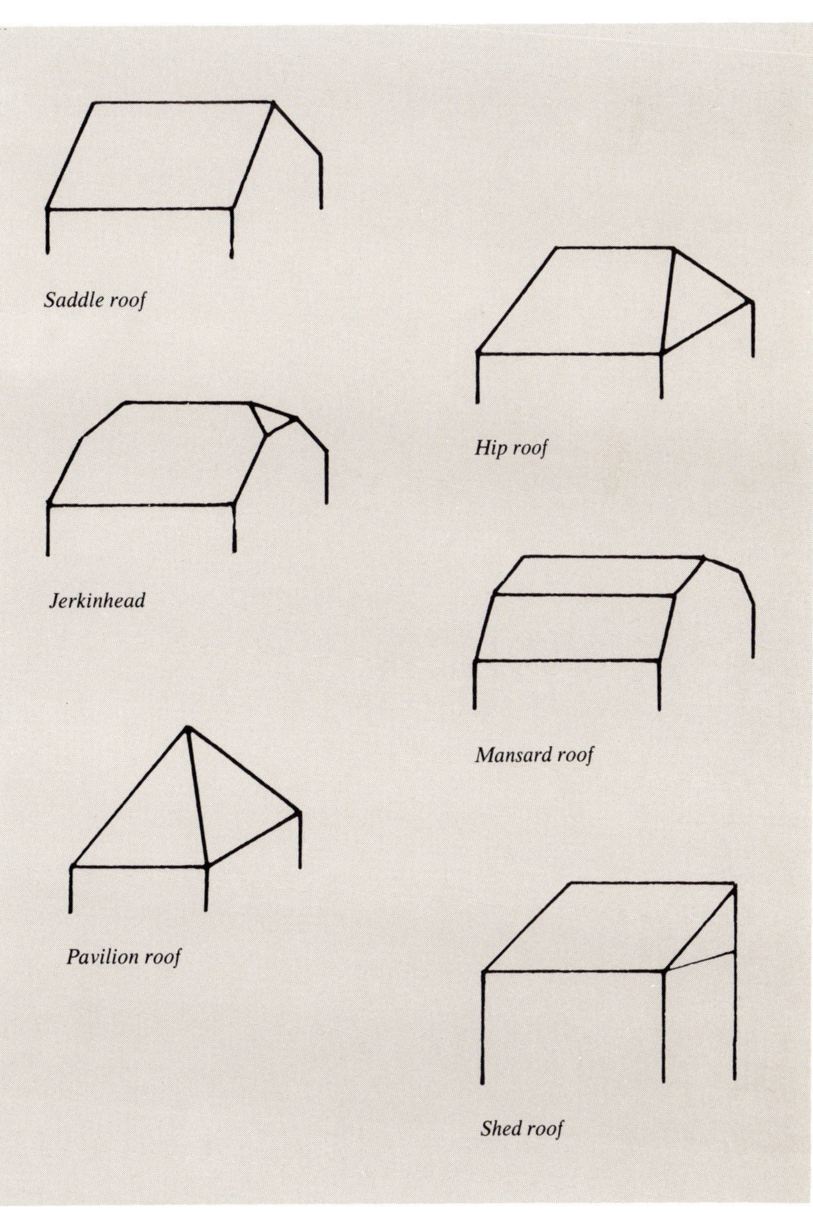

Few old interiors survive and those which do are rarely open to the public. However, a number of old houses have been converted into museums, for example the Simon van Gijn Museum in Dordrecht, the Overijssel Museum in Zwolle, 'De Moriaan' Municipal Museum in Gouda, the Theatre Museum in Amsterdam, the Dutch Costume Museum in The Hague and the Amstelkring Museum (left).

There are also various museums in which the rooms have been decorated and furnished in the style of a particular period – with period furniture, utensils and wall coverings. They can be found in the Rijksmuseum in Amsterdam, the Municipal Museum in The Hague, the Central Museum in Utrecht, 'Het Catharinagasthuis' Municipal Museum in Gouda, 'Het Princessehof' Municipal Museum in Leeuwarden and the Museum of Antiquities in Groningen. The first three museums also have a few very beautiful late 17th and 18th century dolls' houses which give quite a good idea of how the rich furnished their homes at this time.

A lot of information about old interiors can be gained from etchings and paintings. The wash drawing by Willem Buytewech (below) depicts an early 17th century interior, which shows that one and the same room was used for living, sleeping, cooking and eating.

Family round the hearth, wash drawing by Willem Buytewech (1617).

17th century interior, Amstelkring Museum, Oudezijds Voorburgwal 40, Amsterdam.

In 1681 Wilhelmus van Goeree wrote in his discourse, 'Architecture in Ancient and Modern Times': 'The façades should have an air of stately grandeur which is representative of the interior and the inhabitants'. Architects therefore paid a lot of attention to the façades of houses as this was the first impression visitors gained of a household. Mouldings and decorations were added to the doors, windows, and above all to the gables, to make them all the more striking. The photographs show some of the ways in which architects have worked over the past few centuries.

Melkmarkt 10, Zwolle (approx. 1500).

Brink 102, Deventer (1735).

Below left: Bartolotti House Herengracht 170-172, Amsterdam (approx. 1617), after renovation.

Below: Nieuwendijk 11, Flushing (1641).

Right: Peperstraat 6, 's-Hertogenbosch (approx. 1840).

Below right: Westhaven 63, Gouda (approx. 1780).

Oudehaven 54, Zierikzee (1735).

Markt 39-41, 's-Hertogenbosch (approx. 1840-1850).

Alexanderstraat 19-23, The Hague (approx. 1860).

Ceintuurbaan 251-255, Amsterdam (approx. 1880).

Below: Laan van Meerdervoort, The Hague (1904).

Above: Damrak 62. Amsterdam (1886).

The Schröder house (below) built in Utrecht in 1924 and designed by G. T. Rietveld, brings us from traditional to modern architecture. The principal features of the building are the regular, flat sections which project beyond each other to form shapes of different size, the total absence of decoration, the large panes of glass and the use of white and primary colours. Although this house was built of brick and has wooden frames, it is essentially modern in conception. The Schröder house is the most recent example of a house which is preserved as a historic building.

Schröder House, Prins Hendriklaan 50, Utrecht (1924).

Castles and

Country Houses

Horn Castle, near Roermond, a thirteenth-century castle with the protecting towers typical of the period, but with a circular wall betraying its earlier origins. The residential wing was extended in the fifteenth century at the expense of the wall, absorbing the original gatehouse (centre left), which was replaced by the one adjoining it. In this eighteenth century drawing the circular wall (right) is still intact.

Above: The 'Burcht' in Leiden, the oldest part of which probably dates from the twelfth century, stands on a mound erected in the tenth or eleventh century. A circular, battlemented wall, it never contained permanent buildings as the viscount who governed the fortress for the Count of Holland lived elsewhere. (Reproduction of a drawing in the Municipal Archives, Leiden).

Below left: A bird's-eye view of Horn Castle, showing the circular wall, which was partially dismantled in the nineteenth century for the view: the parapet supported by two series of arches is clearly visible. Once the seat of the famous Count of Horn who, together with the Count of Egmond, was beheaded in Brussels in 1568. The castle was damaged by fire in 1948 and restored between 1954 and 1957.

Above: Muiderslot, built shortly after 1280 by Count Floris V of Holland as a military stronghold, has belonged to the state ever since. From 1609 to 1647 it was the official residence of the poet P. C. Hooft in his capacity as Bailiff. It is a good example of the type of square castle with angle towers which was introduced in the thirteenth century, though it was completely rebuilt in the fourteenth century. The low battlemented wall in the foreground protects the court: to the right, the machicolated gatehouse, with the living quarters at the rear. The battlements and arrow slits were reinstated during the restoration carried out between 1895 and 1910.

There are numerous castles in the Netherlands and many historic buildings often referred to as castles which are really country houses. Then as now, town-dwellers built houses in the country, either simply to enjoy the countryside or to run their estates. The history of these country houses cannot be viewed separately from that of the castles that preceded them and this chapter is therefore devoted to both.

Many castles and country houses are protected under the Monuments and Historic Building Act. While representing only a small proportion of the 40,000 or so listed buildings, their importance to our cultural heritage and their contribution to the quality of life are of great significance. The Netherlands is a small country with a population in excess of fourteen million; just as in many other countries, the relics of the past are of inestimable value in establishing our national identity and serving as a link with previous generations. We must therefore do everything we can to ensure that this aspect of our common heritage is cherished and preserved.

The word 'castle' evokes images of scenes from the 'romantic' Middle Ages – gallant knights in shining armour, interminable sieges and fierce battles. In reality, however, the period was anything but romantic. The castles inhabited by mediaeval lords were grim, damp, draughty edifices of stone (window panes were still unknown), with damp, dripping walls.

On the rare occasions when castles were besieged the defenders seldom held out long; in most cases they surrendered at once.

Croy Castle, Stiphout, North Brabant, prior to its restoration. One of the best remaining examples of a late mediaeval castle, it has richly ornamented walls and many prestigious towers, but was indefensible. The oldest section (right) dates from the first decades of the fifteenth century, the rest from ca. 1500. The inner court filled up with buildings in the seventeenth century.

Above left: Doornenburg Castle, near Bemmel. A simple, square structure without corner towers, but with a massive barbican and a chapel in 14-century style. The turrets were added after the inner court had filled up with residential wings in the Middle Ages. Destroyed in 1945, it was later rebuilt according to the original plan. On the right, the barbican with projecting tower and the chapel which escaped destruction in 1945.

Below left: Lunenburg, near Neerlangbroek. A moated 14th-century residential tower, the simplest kind of fortified residence, with each floor consisting of one room. From 1866 until its radical restoration between 1968 and 1971 it formed part of a house which was partly destroyed during the war and later demolished.

What then precisely is a castle?

The word castle covers edifices of many different kinds, which share a common origin in fortified mediaeval habitations which could also double as garrisons. They were thus both private residences and fortresses.

Castles originated in the eleventh and twelfth centuries, when the absence of any effective central authority strengthened the position of the great nobles and landowners, whose relationship gradually evolved into what became known as the feudal system in many parts of Europe. The less powerful of two individuals, the vassal, untertook service under arms in return for land tenancy (fief) and protection granted by the suzerain, or lord. This involved a hierarchical structure resembling a pyramid, since a lord was often both the suzerain of one or more vassals and himself the vassal of a more important lord. Within the system an important role was played by a class of military professionals – the knights, who originally did not belong to the nobility.

A castle was either the residence of a lord and his administrative seat or a purely military stronghold under the control of the monarch; in the latter case it was commanded by a castellan, or governor. Many of the lesser nobility and knights could manage nothing more than a kind of manorhouse of stone which was practically indefensible, despite the moat encircling it. In areas not dominated by great lords or where feudalism had not gained a hold, such as in the three most northerly provinces of the Netherlands, few 'real' castles were built.

The thirteenth and fourteenth centuries marked the peak of traditional castles since subsequently the rise of the towns, the use of mercenary armies and the invention of firearms rendered them obsolete. The power of kings and princes grew afresh, while the knights lost their professional status and became a hereditary class, which merged with the nobility.

In the Late Middle Ages (the fifteenth and sixteenth centuries) a new kind of castle came into being; while retaining the appearance of a castle to mark the status of the owner, notably towers, it was in fact simply a nobleman's residence. Possession of such a seat conferred the right of membership of the governing body of the region. At the beginning of the period, purely military castles, though by then extremely costly, were still built by monarchs.

Hasselholt, Ohé en Laak (Limburg), a late mediaeval nobleman's house with none of the characteristics of a castle. The original building consisted solely of the right wing (early 16th century; the rear wall was rebuilt in the 17th century). The left wing dates from 1629.

Wijchen Castle, built on the site of a mediaeval castle between 1609 and 1626 as a princely country residence for the daughter of William the Silent and her husband, Emanuel de Bragança, pretender to the Portuguese throne. Three wings with large windows and a smaller gatehouse wing surround a courtyard; though encircled by a moat and featuring towers and turrets it is not even remotely fortified. Destroyed by fire in 1906, it was rebuilt and has served as a town hall since 1933.

The 'status' castle went out of fashion in the seventeenth century, and the nobleman's residence came more and more to resemble the country houses then being built by wealthy townsmen. Practically the only reminder of the past was the title 'castle' which such buildings still bore. In some districts, such as Limburg and Utrecht, the old traditions were not abandoned so easily, however, and the nobility continued to cling to the architectural style favoured by their forebears.

In the nineteenth century, there was renewed interest in the Middle Ages and castles, as a result of the Romantic Revival; symbolic towers were added to seventeenth and eighteenth century mansions and new country houses were built in the same style so they could be called – quite erroneously – castles.

Sieges

In times of war the strength of a castle was put to the test. If an attack was imminent all able-bodied men in the service of the lord, whatever their trade or craft, withdrew behind the castle walls and were issued with arms.
If the castle belonged to the monarch or to a vassal who was obliged to place it at the disposal of his suzerain, soldiers were sent to reinforce the garrison. The drawbridge was raised and the occupants awaited the arrival of the enemy.

Hoensbroek Castle, near Roermond, from the rear, showing the 14th-century tower with its 17th-century pointed roof; the adjoining section with large windows dates from the eighteenth century; to the right of it is the projecting chapel.

Hoensbroek Castle. The work of reconstruction on the original foundations within the old double moat began in 1640. The 14th-century round tower was left standing as evidence of its manorial past. The double forecourt is an interesting detail.

Hardenbroek, near Driebergen, is an aristocratic residence which acquired its present appearance in the latter half of the eighteenth century. It is one of the most notable examples of the predilection of Utrecht noblemen for towers as an expression of their status: surrounded by a moat, the house was also embellished with pointed roof sections at the angles, symbolic towers out of harmony with the architectural style of the building.

The besiegers brought with them impressive engines of war: siege towers with platforms to reach the battlements, battering rams to force open the gates and assault devices such as trebuchets and spingals to hurl rocks, balls of flaming pitch and even rotting corpses in the hope of infecting the defenders with disease.

The defenders did not sit idly by during the onslaught. Archers shot volleys of arrows through the narrow slits and any of the attacking force who managed to fight their way to the foot of the walls were assailed with showers of rocks and boiling oil through the machicolations – the openings along the base of the parapets.

If the assailants failed to take the castle by storm, they could resort to blocking off all outside sources of supply and starving the defenders out. Sieges were rare occurrences, however, nor did the defenders often hold out to the last man: as contemporary manuscripts tell us, they usually surrendered with surprising alacrity.

Weldam Castle, near Goor. The first section, a rectangular house in the Classical style, was built on the site of a mediaeval manor house in 1644: two transverse wings were later added to the front. Encircled by a wide moat, and with a forecourt flanked by outbuildings, the structure, still towerless at that time, clearly went back several centuries; the towers at the rear were added in the late nineteenth century. The French-style gardens were laid out in 1886 by the Parisian E. André, and the surrounding park in English style gradually took shape during the 18th-20th centuries. (Photograph taken in 1927.)

Middachten, near De Steeg (Gelderland), built in 1694-1697 by Steven Vennecool on the site of a mediaeval castle, is an example of the severe architectural style of the time. The moat and the barbican, or outwork, form a separate island; one of the outbuildings dates from the sixteenth century, betraying its origin as a castle.

Middachten Castle near De Steeg (Gelderland); the staircase (right) and the ceiling (above).

Types of castles

Fortified castles
The development of the castle kept pace with assault and defence tactics, but was closely linked with the traditions of military architecture evolved in previous centuries. Circular and rectangular fortresses with earthwork ramparts and a separate forecourt around which workshops were grouped, had long been in existence. The keep, or donjon, was inherited from Roman and eastern military architecture. The earliest castles were round and were not used as habitations.
The type consisting of a walled artificial mound surmounted by a keep – built first of wood and later of stone – came from France. An example of an English variation with a circular inner wall instead of a keep, the 'Burcht', still survives in Leiden (page 52).
The Netherlands is extremely flat and contains countless rivers and waterways; a special type of castle developed – of which Teilingen Castle, near Sassenheim, is a good example – with a moated circular wall but no central mound. The habitable keep added later was an element imported from France.

The Crusaders brought back with them new ideas based on the more advanced military architecture of the Middle East. One such innovation introduced in the thirteenth century consisted of towers projecting from the walls which meant that the

Henkenshage Castle, St. Oedenrode, was built as it stands, complete with towers, gateway and battlements, in the nineteenth century, a product of the Romantic Revival. Note the size of the castle in relation to the surrounding trees.

Right: Goudestein, near Maarssen, was built c. 1620 by Johan Huydecoper, Burgomaster of Amsterdam. The first of the country houses along the river Vecht, it was a modest house adjacent to his tenant's farm set in the middle of an orchard. (Bird's eye drawing by Floris van Berckenrode, 1628; Van der Muelen family archives.)

defenders were not exposed to return fire, but at the same time had an unimpeded view of the attackers' movements at the foot of the walls.

The more or less square type of castle with circular or square towers at the four corners, such as Brederode Castle near Santpoort, Ammersoyen Castle near Ammerzoden in Gelderland (in its original state) and Muiderslot Castle (page 53), also date from this period.

The living quarters were situated along one or more sides of the inner bailey, while the workshops, stables and other offices were in the forecourt. Natural mounds and hills provided sites for massive strongholds. Needless to say, constructions of this kind had to be adapted to the contours of the terrain, which meant that their form was often irregular. Some, however, were encircled by double walls, with the approach to the gateway in between, thus exposing assailants' unprotected right flank to heavy cross fire. The sole example of such a castle in the Netherlands, Valkenburg Castle, is now in ruins.

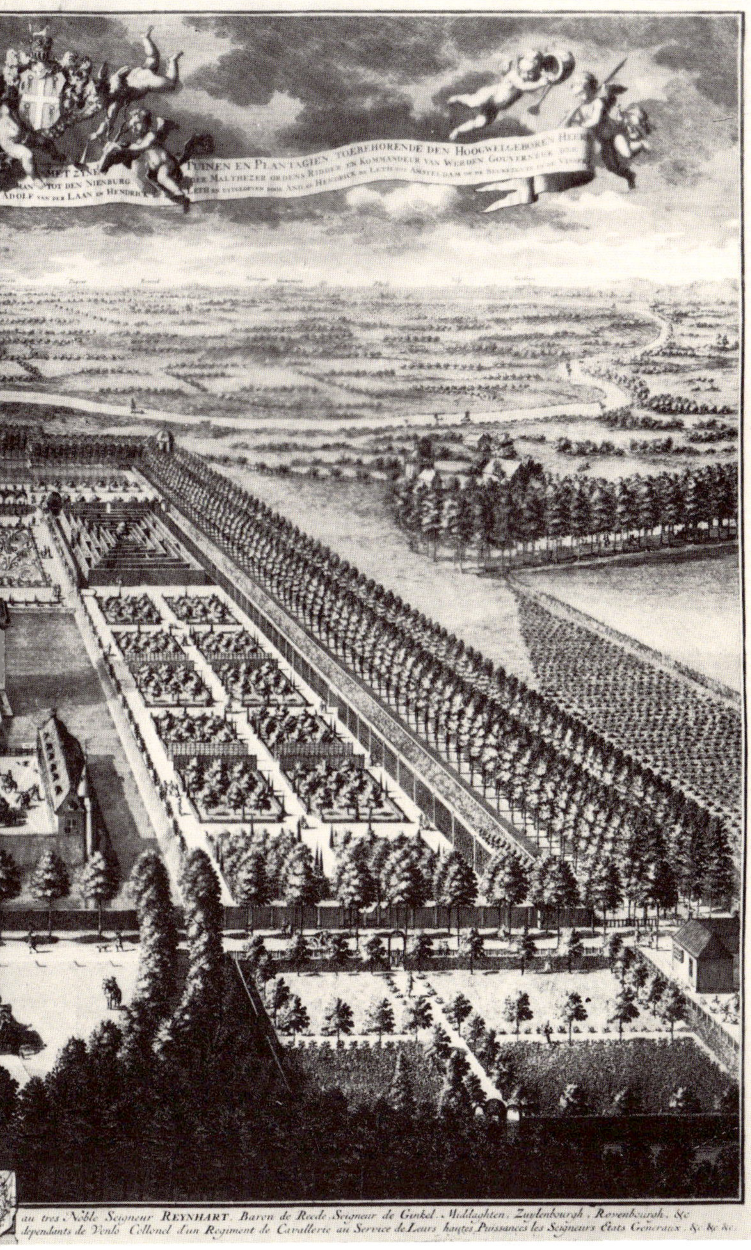

Middachten, De Steeg. Reconstructed between 1694 and 1697, the house is surrounded by large formal gardens laid out in accordance with the fashion of the time in rectangular sections allowing an uninterrupted view from the house of an ornamented parterre, a pond and a pergola of clipped trees. Mazes of high hedges are on each side. Of Middachten's treelined lanes, the main alley was famous; its centuries old trees were felled during the war, but have since been replaced. (Print: A. v.d. Laan and H. de Leth.)

There were, of course, numerous simplified forecourt versions of the ideal castle, like Doornenburg Castle near Bemmel (page 54), built without towers but with an extensive forecourt. Some of the castles erected then and later were of an outdated circular design, probably because they were built on the foundations of an earlier structure, such as Horn Castle, near Roermond (page 50-52), and Bergh Castle, 's-Heerenberg (page 64).
The simplest type of castle which was both fortified and habitable was the square or rectangular tower, frequently found in the northern provinces and the Utrecht region, where several are still standing. Most of them date from the fourteenth century and were in no way military strongholds built to house garrisons.

Status castles

When it was no longer necessary to build castles for defence purposes, since the development of sophisticated weapons had made it impossible to defend them, castle-builders devoted more attention to comfort, and exteriors became less forbidding. Walls were no longer so massive and ornamentation and large windows appeared in outside walls, which would formerly have been vulnerable to attack. Croy Castle near Stiphout (page 55) is an example of this type, with elegant gables and steeple-like embrasured towers dating from the fifteenth century. Maurik Castle in Vught resembles a small palace with charming corbelled turrets. Keppel Castle and Wychen Castle (page 56) were built in the same Renaissance style in the early seventeenth century. Wherever possible, remains of a castle's martial past were retained as proof of its pedigree. Hoensbroek Castle (1640) in Limburg (page 57), though featuring many elements of the past, including a double moat, two forecourts, towers and an inner bailey, was nevertheless a modern palace in its day with a fourteenth-century keep as a reminder of its mediaeval origins.

Oostermeer, view of the garden from the house.

Left: Rupelmonde, Nieuwersluis, one of the most beautiful houses along the Vecht. Built in the seventeenth century and remodelled in its present form in the eighteenth century. The principal rooms, including a projecting drawing room, faced the river, as was the case with most of these houses.

St. Jan ter Heere, near Domburg, an eighteenth century country house which no longer exists, with high hedges and trees clipped into exotic shapes. All country houses were once surrounded by such gardens. (Engraving by J. Arends, 1777; collection of Zeeuws Genootschap, Middelburg.)

Above: Bergh Castle, 's-Heerenberg.

Below: Oostermeer, near Ouderkerk on the river Amstel, was built in 1728. The garden, laid out early in the present century by Leonard Springer, combines elements of the formal French style and the English landscape style with eighteenth-century statues.

Castles built in the form of country houses

Architectural tastes changed by the mid-seventeenth century; the accent shifted to severe, regular structures and towers went out of favour. The aristocracy, whose way of life was increasingly similar to that of the wealthy merchant class, rebuilt their castles as rectangular houses with imposing roofs, but kept the world at a distance by means of moats and forecourts, as can still be seen at Amerongen (1676), Middachten (1695) near De Steeg (page 59, 61) and Eerde (1715) near Ommen. Traces of the tower lingered on only in Utrecht and Limburg, as in Renswoude Castle (1645) and Hillenraad Castle (1767) near Swalmen.

The nineteenth and twentieth centuries: romantic castles

The mid-nineteenth century revival of interest in castles produced not only the addition of mock ramparts, etc. to real castles but also residential towers (Sandenburg Castle near Neerlangbroek) and even complete castles like Henkenshage Castle in St. Oedenrode (page 60).
Typical of this period was the resurrection as a fairy-tale castle in 1892 and succeeding years of De Haar Castle, Vleuten, which had been deserted for centuries. The character of many fine country houses like Weldam, Goor (page 58) and Oud-Poelgeest, Oegstgeest, was radically altered by the addition of towers and turrets. Entirely new 'castles' – Oud Wassenaar and Wittenburg in Wassenaar, Duin en Kruidberg near Santpoort, Hoge Vuursche near Baarn and Sint Hubertus near Otterlo – came into being complete with towers to justify their denomination as 'castles'. The First World War put an end to the construction of castles and, unless there is a new period of feudalism in the future, that chapter of history is closed for good.

Huis Duivenvoorde, Voorschoten, entrance-hall.

's-Graveland, park gates of Gooilust.

Loenen a.d. Vecht. 18th-century summer house with characteristic domed roof. It was the custom to retire to such buildings to take tea and admire the view. They were also used as boat houses as the door at water level indicates.

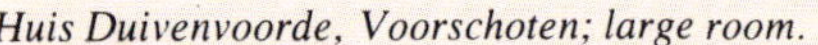

Huis Duivenvoorde, Voorschoten; large room.

Huis Mattenburg near Woensdrecht, a dignified country house with a white stuccoed exterior dating from the third quarter of the 19th century.

What is a country house?

The term country house is usually taken to mean a house built in the country by a town-dweller wishing to enjoy the peace and tranquility of country life. The origins of this type of residence in the Netherlands were very modest.
Early in the seventeenth century, when the ravages of the Eighty Years' War were virtually no longer felt within the country and money was pouring into the new Republic via the East India Company, wealthy burghers began to invest their money in land. The farmhouses they built were let to tenant farmers, but they reserved for themselves a 'gentleman's room' where they stayed from time to time to keep an eye on things and in so doing developed a taste for country life.

Before long the houses built as summer residences had grown in size and comfort until they dwarfed the original farmhouses. The surrounding land was likewise transformed; orchards and kitchen gardens were reduced to make way for pleasure gardens and parks, although they did not disappear altogether; the hardheaded Dutchman was too practical not to harvest the fruits of his labours in both senses of the word.

Country residences were built along the Amstel and Vecht rivers and along the foot of the Kennemer dunes. A second type dates back to the twelve-year truce (1609-1621) in the Eight Years' War, when many Catholic noblemen who had left the country long ago disposed of their castles and estates. The new owners gladly acquired the titles that went with the estates. In form and character the castles of the aristocracy came more and more to resemble country houses, even though, unlike the latter, they were occupied by their owners all year round.
Nowadays, with transport no longer a problem, owners can reside in their country houses permanently and the distinction between the two categories has become blurred. Residence for part of the year has been replaced by the use of weekend houses which, however, lack the land that formed the second characteristic of the country house, and therefore fall outside this category.

Later, the second feature wealthy merchants' country houses and the seats of the nobility had in common was that both were surrounded by gardens.
Formally laid out parks were practically unknown in the Netherlands before 1650; the remarkable gardens of Elswout, a house in Overveen dating from approximately 1640, are an exception. It was not until 1680 or thereabouts that French and Italian inspired formal parks and gardens centering on the house came fully into their own, with walks, avenues, ornamental lakes, ponds and groves laid out symmetrically in geomatrical patterns on a straight axis.

Lawns alternated with parterres which made decorative patterns with box hedges and coloured pebbles. Fanciful topiary and high hedges, statues and urns completed the formal garden in which nature was subservient to the decorative style of the interior of the house: house and park together formed one complete whole.

The formal garden has now disappeared almost without trace, for in the second half of the eighteenth century a new fashion was imported from England which was its exact opposite. Parks were now laid out in the form of an idealised natural landscape with flowing lines, asymmetrical contours and trees left to grow naturally.
In fact it was highly contrived: the winding ornamental lakes, the lawns, the woods and the copses were all carefully planned to produce special effects and views both of the house and from it.
This 'natural' style of landscaping was introduced into the Netherlands by J. G. Michaël and remained popular throughout the nineteenth century, largely through Michaël's successors, a family of landscape gardeners named Zocher. Others whose work was influential were H. and S. A. van Lunteren and L. P. Roodbaard in the north.

Riniastate in Oudemirdum (Friesland). A small country house of this type is practically indistinguishable from a villa. Built by T. Romein in 1843, its white stucco exterior stands out in pleasing contrast with the trees in the surrounding park.

Huis Mattenburg near Woensdrecht, view of the park in the English style where groups of trees and ornamental ponds mingle to suggest a natural landscape.

Low-lying areas near rivers and canals had been popular in the previous century, but preference was now given to more elevated sandy areas like that immediately east of Utrecht (Utrechtse Heuvelrug) and the Veluwe district. Some features contrary to the principle of the natural landscape, such as avenues of trees and, in summer, rows of orange trees in tubs, still held their own, and soon a longing for more colour prompted the addition of flower beds. Round 1880 there was a revival of interest in the formal style of the previous century and fine gardens of this type were laid out by the Frenchman Edouard André and by H. A. C. Poortman. The parks and gardens designed from then on were usually a combination of formal and landscape elements. Well-known in the early part of the present century were Leonard Springer and the Copijn family, who are still active today.

De Schaffelaar, Barneveld. The present house, built in 1852 by A. van Veggel, replaces an earlier manor house; as it is not on exactly the same site, there is no moat to indicate its older origins. Its English Neo-Gothic style is reflected in such details as the bay windows, which were popular in England at that time. The tower, which had to be demolished because of its dilapidated condition, was rebuilt during the recent restoration.

Hofwijck, built on the Vliet canal at Voorburg in 1641-1642 by Pieter Post for the statesman Constantijn Huygens. Though modest in size, its moat reflects the vanity of its owner by suggesting noble origins. It is now the Huygens Museum.

Churches

The Monuments and Historic Buildings Act provides for the protection of buildings which are at least 50 years old and which are important for aesthetic, historical or cultural reasons. Almost 2400 churches in the Netherlands are listed under the act.

The churches tend to play a key role in determining the character or atmosphere of a village or town since they dominate by virtue of their size, architectural style of the materials used in their construction.

This chapter is primarily concerned with the architecture of churches but also deals with their function as places of worship since the two aspects are closely related.

We hope that it will convey something of the unique character of historic Dutch churches and at the same time serve as a practical guide to visitors.

Sandstone relief, Peter's Church, Utrecht.

Left: St. Michael's Church, Zwolle.

The oldest churches

The Gospel was first preached in the Netherlands by missionaries who built churches in styles derived from their own countries. The single-roomed church with a narrow straight-ended choir at Lemiers in Limburg (right) is a late example (possibly as late as the 11th century) of a type of church introduced in the 8th century from Northumbria in the north of England by St. Willibrord. *Room* here refers to a single undivided space while *choir* (or *chancel*) denotes the area at the east end containing the altar.

The Church at Lemiers: single-roomed church with a narrow straight-ended choir (11th or 12th century). Oldest type of church in the Netherlands.

St. Peter's, Utrecht. Romanesque church from the 11th century.

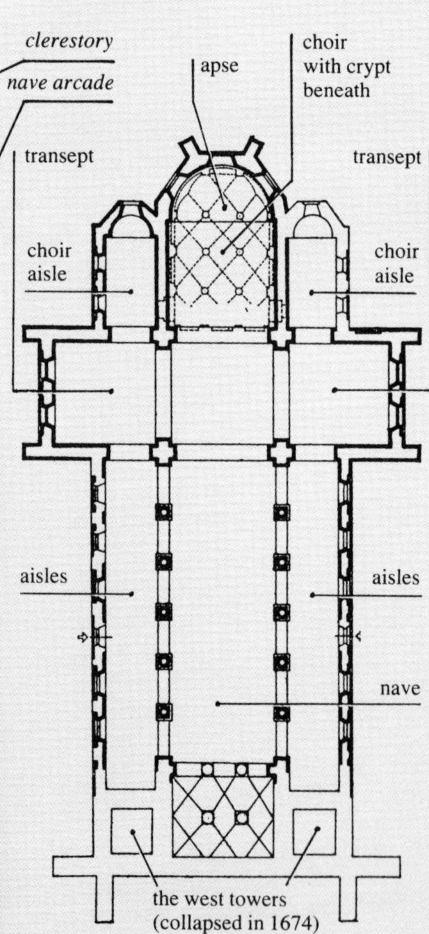

Above: Reconstructed plan of St. Peter's, Utrecht

Romanesque churches

11th and 12th century churches were built in the Romanesque style, characterised by features such as heavy walls and small windows with rounded arches. St. Peter's, Utrecht (below left), built in the 11th century, is a basilica, a common type of design during the Middle Ages characterised by a nave which is illuminated by a row of windows above columns. The cushion capitals in the nave which make an easy transition from the round columns to the square corners of the wall between two semi-circular arches are typically Romanesque. The plan of the church is in the form of a cross, the symbolism of which is obvious. Later Gothic forms can be seen in window tracery and the dark-coloured ribs of the vaults in the choir, which is raised to accommodate a crypt underneath. This is another typically Romanesque feature which originated in the ancient custom of keeping the relics of saints in a room under the altar where they could be worshipped by the faithful. The crypt of the Church of St. Lebuin in Deventer (below) was built during the episcopate of Bishop Bernulphus of Utrecht, who built St. Peter's. Cushion capitals can be seen on the elaborately carved columns here too. Romanesque groin vaulting is also clearly visible; in fact it consists of a series of intersections at right angles of two tunnel vaults which are the shape of a rounded arch, rather like a cylinder cut lengthways. Groin vaulting is therefore only possible over a square bay with the result that Romanesque churches often consist of a series of adjoining square bays.

Crypt under the choir of St. Lebuin, Deventer (11th century).

groin vaulting

shaft of the column

spiral patterning on shaft

base

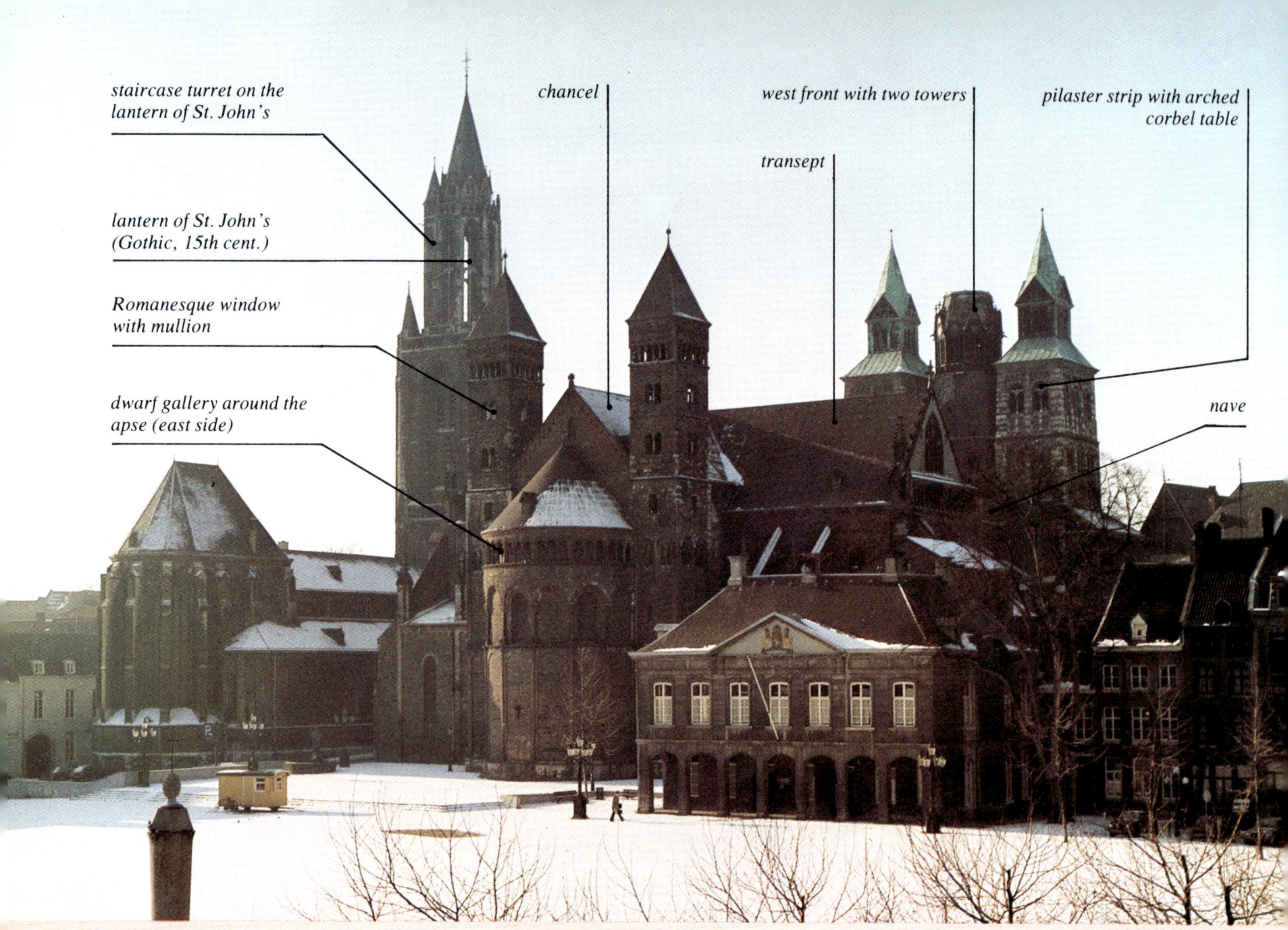

staircase turret on the lantern of St. John's

chancel

west front with two towers

pilaster strip with arched corbel table

transept

lantern of St. John's (Gothic, 15th cent.)

Romanesque window with mullion

dwarf gallery around the apse (east side)

nave

St. Gervase's Maastricht from the north-east. On the left in the photograph is St. John's (Gothic).

Churches were often built where saints were buried, such as St. Gervase's, the important Romanesque church in Maastricht (above) built on the site of the 4th century grave of St. Gervase.
The oldest part of the building dates from the 11th century while the 12th century Romanesque parts may be recognized by the pilaster strips, vertical courses (or lesenes) linked by an arched corbel table, by the bays with two lights and by the dwarf gallery round the apse, the semi-circular projection from the choir.
The west of the church (with its two towers) is a typically Carolingian feature and is constructed in a way which suggests that it had a special function or significance, although we do not know precisely what that was. Traditionally it would have been assigned a role connected with pastoral care, ecclesiastical justice or temporal power.

St. Gervase's Church, Maastricht, cloister.

Bierum church, Groningen Province (13th century).

A smaller type of west choir is to be found in the northern provinces of the Netherlands. The 13th-century church at Bierum (right) has a choir above a vaulted crypt under its tower but in this case the western end has a different significance.
Mediaeval churches are orientated with the chancel facing east towards Jerusalem. The west was regarded as belonging to the devil, so an altar was often placed there dedicated to St. Michael, the conqueror of evil. The heavy buttress was built at a later date to prevent the tower from collapsing.

Gothic churches

The Gothic style was introduced from France in the 13th century and developed a number of variations as a result of different foreign influences. The choir of Utrecht Cathedral (page 76) was inspired by French Classic Gothic and was begun in 1254, when the Romanesque precursor of the present cathedral was still standing. Construction started in the east, where the choir, the most important part of the church, is located. The Romanesque church was gradually demolished as the new building progressed. It was a costly undertaking which took a long time to complete: the choir lantern (clerestory) was not finished until a hundred years later.
Gothic architecture is based on the creation of lofty spaces to which as much light as possible is admitted, but the vaulting exerts tremendous pressure on the walls, which contain large numbers of windows. The

Utrecht Cathedral, view of the choir from the east (13th and 14th century).

Amersfoort, Onze Lieve Vrouwetoren (Our Lady's Tower).

gable surmounted by finial

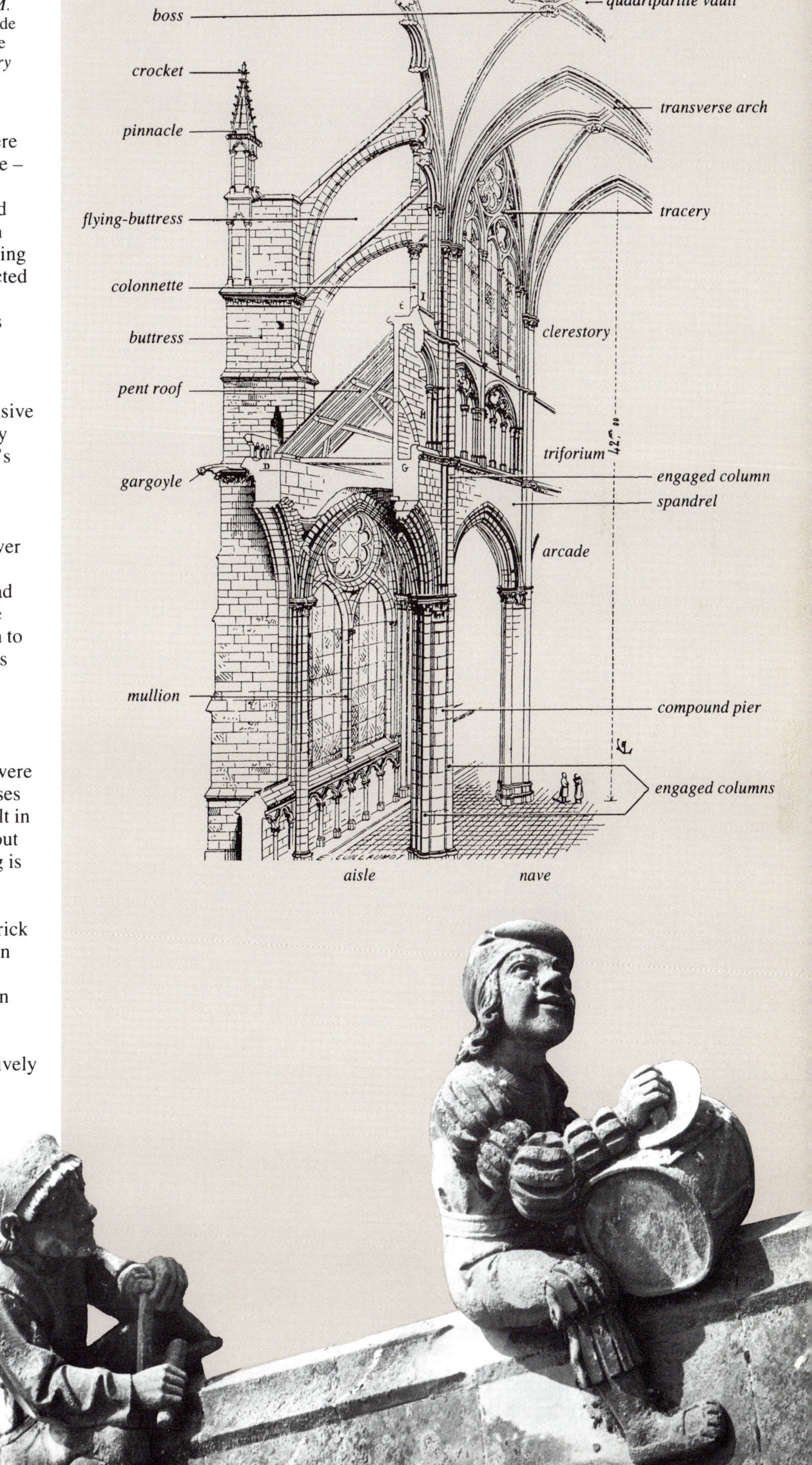

Cross section of a church with stone vaulting and flying buttresses. Engraving from M. Viollet-Le-Duc. Dictionnaire Raisonné de l'Architecture Française du XIe au XVIe siècle, *part 1 (Paris, 1854), p. 203 (entry 'arc').*

materials with which churches were built – brick often faced with stone – were capable of withstanding a considerable amount of downward pressure but less able to cope with outward thrust. Buttresses and flying buttresses were therefore constructed to absorb the pressure exerted on exterior walls; outward thrust was transmitted to the ground via projecting buttresses.

Building a church was both expensive and technically difficult. The early 16th century painting of St. Bavo's Church (or the Grote Kerk) in Haarlem (page 79) served as a relatively cheap model, to give an impression of what the central tower over the crossing of the nave and transept would look like after it had been built. The painting may have been used to publicize a campaign to raise funds to build the tower. This church has no flying buttresses although they were undoubtedly intended, as can be seen from the projecting stones between the windows of the clerestory which were designed to join the flying buttresses to the wall. It is impossible to vault in brick in a church of this size without flying buttresses; *wooden* vaulting is therefore used in the nave.

It was due to lack of money that brick vaulting was abandoned here but in some cases it was not possible on technical grounds, especially when the church was built on peaty soil which cannot support heavy buildings, and in view of the relatively primitive mediaeval methods of making foundations.

St. John's Church, 's-Hertogenbosch; figures on arch.

The Middle Ages

There are different sorts of mediaeval churches, but each one contains an altar at which the Mass was celebrated. The Mass is the most important sacrament which takes place in a church since the bread and the wine are continual reminders of Christ's passion and the salvation of mankind.

The *chapel* is the lowest in order of importance among the various types of church. It is a small place of prayer without a regular priest of its own.

A *parish church*, which often started life as a chapel before it had sufficient parishioners to justify the appointment of a priest, served a particular district or parish.

A *collegiate church* was one to which several priests or cannons were attached. Together they formed a *chapter* which was like a monastic community except that its members did not actually live a community life. They said the 'hours', services at appointed times of day at which certain prescribed prayers were recited and sacred texts were sung.

The plan of St. James' Church in The Hague (below right) gives a good idea of the lay-out of a mediaeval church. The high altar, dedicated to the church's patron saint, stands against the back wall of the choir. In front of the altar (marked P on the plan) are the stalls for the canons which would have been carved (See illustration of choir stalls in St. Martin's, Bolsward). The choir of St. James' was enclosed on all sides by a rail or screen. The area around the choir, the ambulatory, enables visitors to walk round the church without disturbing the service.

Fifteenth-century choir stalls in St. Martin's Church, Bolsward.

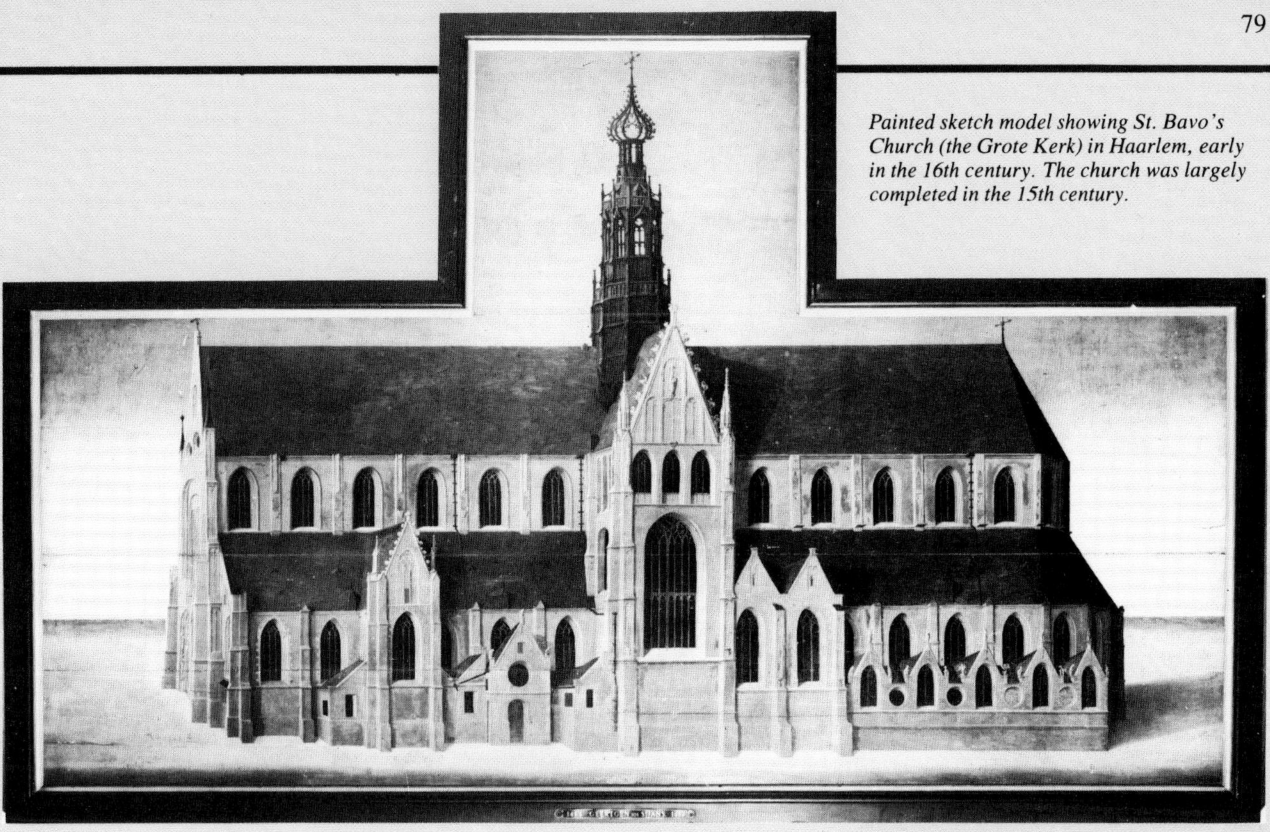

Painted sketch model showing St. Bavo's Church (the Grote Kerk) in Haarlem, early in the 16th century. The church was largely completed in the 15th century.

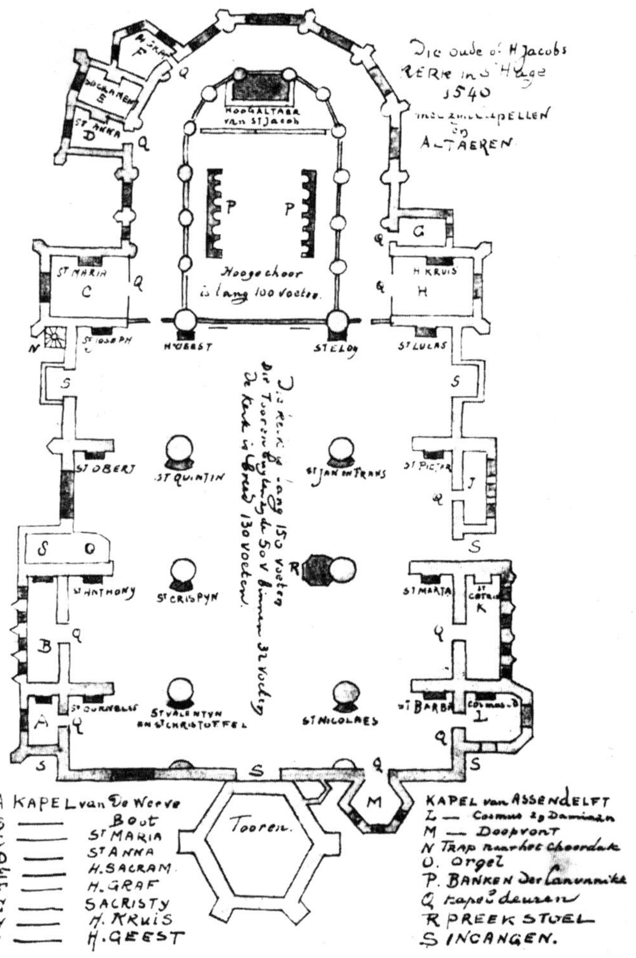

The chancel could also be separated from the nave by means of a *rood loft* or gallery which could also be used to accommodate the choir. The rood loft (shown on page 80) is in St. Cunera's Church in Rhenen and dates from the mid-16th century. It is an interesting example of the early Renaissance style. Although it is rib-vaulted in the Gothic manner, it has other features directly modelled on examples from Italy where the Renaissance style originated.

Another important part of the mediaeval church was the *sacristy* where the vestments and other requisites for the Mass were kept; it was usually on the north side of the choir, but in St. James' it is on the south side (G). The pulpit is in the nave, against a column (R). Baptism of children took place in a separate hexagonal extension near the west tower (M).

Plan of St. James' Church, The Hague. Coloured pen drawing in the Bodel Nijenhuis Collection, Leiden.

The plan (page 79) also shows where several chapels have been added to the church separately. These were often built for the veneration of a particular saint or the Virgin Mary, to whom numerous elaborate Lady Chapels were dedicated, most of them on the north side of the choir.
If a church possessed the relics of a saint they were displayed in a reliquary on a separate altar during festivals. Chapels were also built by guilds, religious societies and private individuals. Altars were also set up against the columns between the nave and the aisles.
The large number of altars was necessary partly because they were regularly used for *requiem masses* which the priest said for the souls of the departed. The length and frequency of the mass depended on the amount of money which had been paid.

The interior of a mediaeval church in use is illustrated in a 15th-century miniature from a Book of Hours. From the crossing we can see into the choir, with its *ambulatory,* in which a bishop is seated before the altar with two acolytes standing on either side of the altar (the one on the right is holding the bishop's crozier). To the right between the choir and the ambulatory are stalls with a canopy: this is the *sedilia,* where the assisting clergy sat during the celebration of the mass.

Behind the altar is the *retable,* enclosing a panel illustrating the crucifixion. The altar itself is raised on a dais with three steps leading up to it. The choir extends over two bays and is enclosed on three sides. At the base of the clerestory windows there is a gallery, indicated by the openings in the walls. The choir arcade is supported by compound piers while the vault itself consists of quadripartite vaults between transverse arches. The priest – in this case a bishop, as the mitre on the right-hand side of the altar indicates – is preaching to the congregation in which there are a number of nuns. There are no seats; the congregation is standing or sitting on stools which they have brought with them.

Rood loft in St. Cunera's, Rhenen (mid-16th century). The figures and reliefs on the parapet have been lost.

Zeddam, R. C. Church, details from retable.

Utrecht, Mariaplaats showing St. Mary's Church; painting by Pieter Saenredam, 1663 (Museum Boymans-van Beuningen, Rotterdam).

The location of the mediaeval church

Until 1559, Utrecht was the only city in the Netherlands which was the seat of a bishop. In the painting by Pieter Saenredam (1663) shown above, three sorts of churches can be seen. In the centre is the tower of the cathedral, the bishop's own church built in the 14th century; by virtue of its importance as the cathedral tower it was used as something of a model in the Middle Ages and was followed by the towers of St. Martin's, Groningen, Our Lady of Amersfoort (page 76) and St. John's, Maastricht (page 74). A tower was important to the whole community as it housed a clock, a look-out post and bells which could be rung to communicate various types of message.

The position of the cathedral can be explained on historical grounds as it was founded within the confines of the Roman *castellum* or fortress which later became a possession of the Frankish kings. The original church was founded around the year 600 under royal protection, hence the choice of a site within the royal estate in Utrecht.

On the left in Saenredam's picture is the tower of the Buurkerk, the earliest parish church in the oldest part of the city, where the townspeople (the 'buren') lived. On the right in the painting is the Romanesque Collegiate Church of St. Mary, demolished in 1813, which, together with St. John's, St. Peter's and St. Paul's (also demolished), formed the shape of a cross, a scheme begun by bishop Bernulphus in the 11th century. The location of these four churches to the north, east and west of the cathedral, was deliberately chosen to give the city a holy and God-fearing aspect.

St. Catharine's Church, Utrecht; interior. Painting by Pieter Saenredam.

St. Mary's Church, Utrecht; interior. Painting by Pieter Saenredam.

Old Church, Amsterdam

Naturally the earliest parish churches were founded where the oldest settlements were and, conversely, the oldest part of a large modern city is to be found in the neighbourhood of the oldest parish church. The Oude Kerk or 'Old Church' in Amsterdam (left) is a good example of this for it is situated just off the Warmoesstraat which follows the line of the dike along the River Amstel, where the first inhabitants built their houses. There was a small chapel in the 13th century to which a priest was attached in 1334; it was eventually replaced by the Oude Kerk, the building of which went on until well into the 16th century.

The twelve-sided Jerusalem Chapel (below) built on to the east of the Grote Kerk (St. John's) in Gouda is important for our knowledge of mediaeval ideas.
It was built in 1504 by a priest who had returned from a pilgrimage to the Holy Land.
Its twelve sides echo the twelve columns in the Church of the Holy Sepulchre in Jerusalem which is circular in shape.

The Jerusalem Chapel, Gouda (1504).

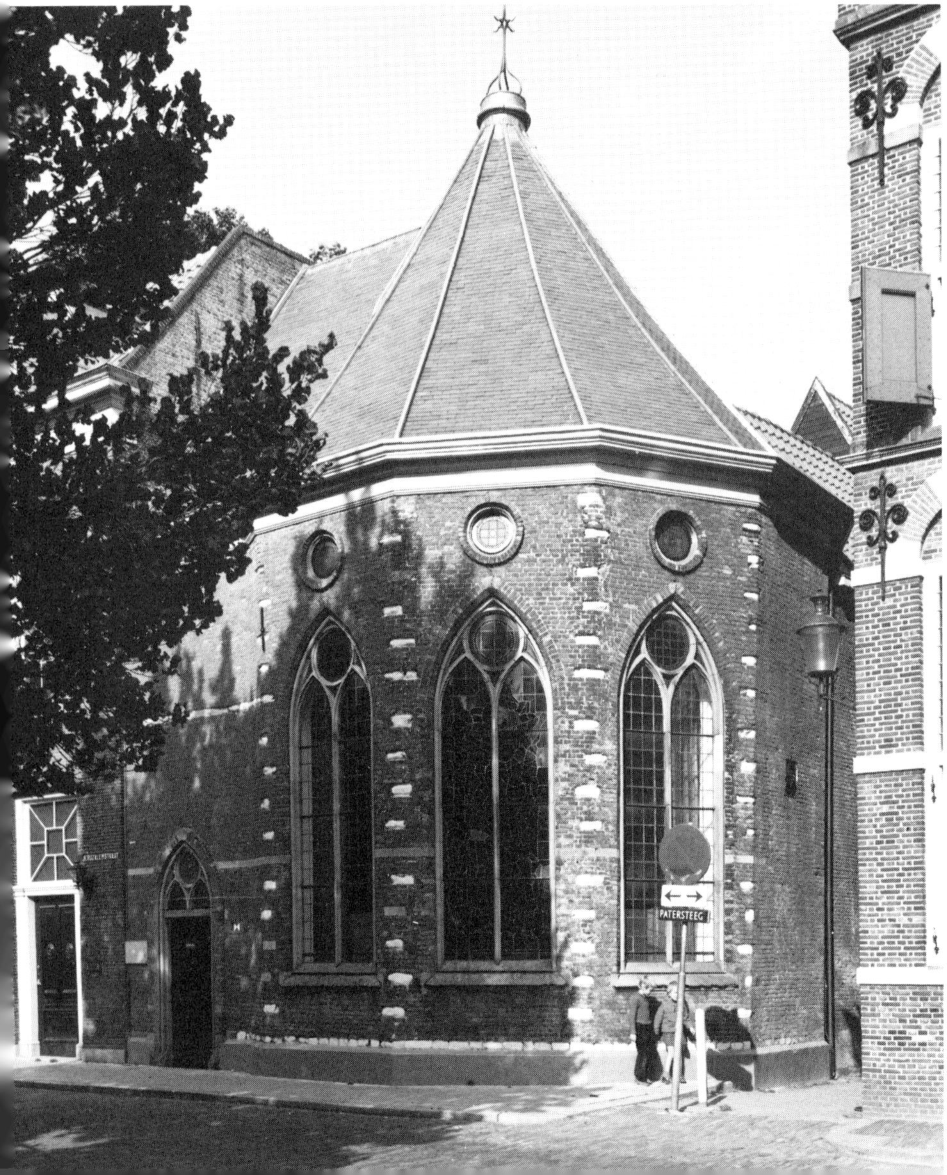

Roman Catholic Churches after the Reformation

Roman Catholism was forbidden in the Netherlands during the revolt against Spain (the Eighty Years' War) and until 1795 Catholics were forced to hold their services in secret. They were eventually allowed their own places of worship on payment of a certain sum, provided they were not visible from a public thoroughfare. The *secret churches* built under this arrangement are often found in an enclosure behind the houses on a street but they could also be inconspicuously incorporated into a row of terraced houses, for example the Church of St. John and St. Ursula in the Béguinage in Amsterdam. In the photograph (above right) of the Nieuwe Zijds Voorburgwal the presence of a church is betrayed by the rounded windows set into the otherwise blank surface.

Catholics in the Generality (those areas in the south of the country which did not form separate provinces but came under the direct control of the States-General, the central government), built a number of *frontier chapels* just across the border, in an area that was not under the control of the States-General so that they might hold services undisturbed. The isolated church of St. Mary Magdelene in Esdonk (below right) dating from the 17th century, is an example of a chapel built on uncultivated land.

The secret Roman Catholic Church of St. John and St. Ursula on the Nieuwezijds Voorburgwal, Amsterdam (view from the street).

The Chapel of St. Mary Magdelene in Esdonk (built in 1695).

Right: Triptych with the Ten Commandments in the Reformed Church, Poortugaal, South Holland (1687).

Below: Seating plan of the Noorderkerk in Amsterdam, a Protestant church built between 1620 and 1623 which gave rise to many others on the same lines, such as the Noorderkerk in Groningen (1665).

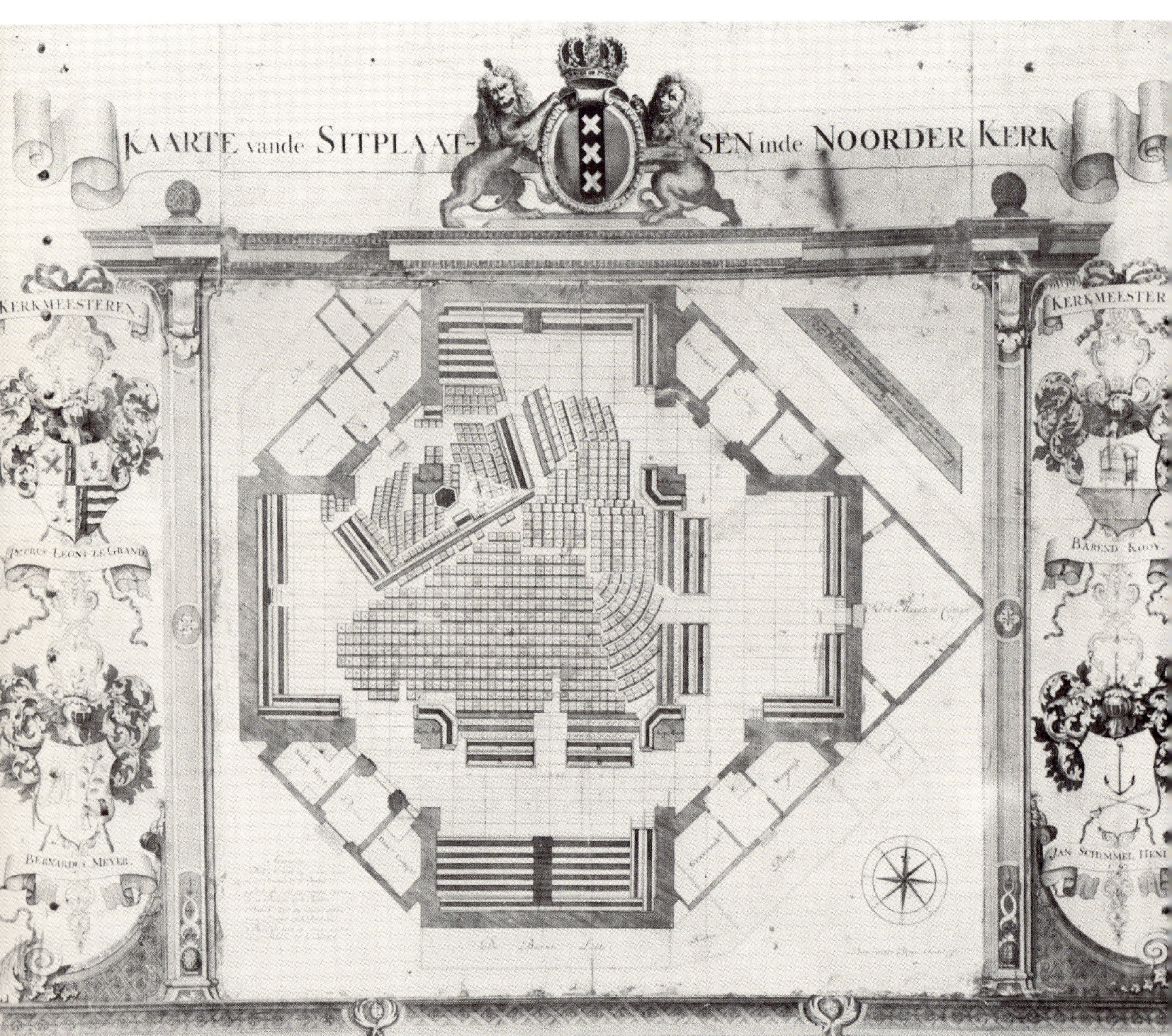

Protestant Churches

The most important churches were built in the 17th century when Protestantism was supported by the government and the building of churches by other denominations was virtually prohibited.

A centralized plan was best for Protestant churches as it enabled the entire congregation to hear the sermon, which played a major role in the service, from all parts of the church. Mediaeval Catholic churches, on the other hand, emphasized the east-west orientation which concentrated the gaze of the congregation in the nave eastwards towards the choir and the high altar.

The Noorderkerk in Amsterdam is typical of the Protestant churches of this period. The plan (above) shows numbered seats facing the pulpit

against the north-western pillar.
The *baptistry* around the pulpit, the liturgical centre of the church, is separated from the rest of the interior by a *baptistry screen.* A similar screen may be seen in the Nieuwe Kerk in The Hague, which dates from the mid-17th century. Baptisms took place there and it was also where the elders of the church had their seats. Whereas the inside of a Catholic church was decorated with pictures of saints, that of a Protestant church was dominated by biblical texts, reflecting the central importance of the Word of God as contained in the Scriptures. Large and sometimes decorated boards with texts, and memorial tablets, are all that is to be found on the whitewashed walls. An example of a board showing the Ten Commandments is to be seen in the Reformed Church in Poortugaal (above).

Protestant churches in use

Seats were necessary because of the long sermons. Some were permanent fixtures, certainly for church officials such as elders, deacons and church-wardens, and the local patrician families would also have their own imposing pews, usually opposite the pulpit.

A painting of about 1655 shows the Nieuwe Zijds Kapel in Amsterdam (below right), a Gothic building (demolished in 1908) which was taken from the Catholics during the Reformation and converted for Protestant services.
On the right is the minister in the pulpit, above which is a large sounding-board to project his voice to the whole congregation. The baptistry is just visible below the pulpit. On the extreme left there are special pews facing the pulpit for the local gentry and some separate seats round the compound pillars between the nave and the aisle. There is also an organ. Communion, the Protestant equivalent of the Mass, was not an essential part of the service; it was celebrated once every two or three months at a long table placed next to the baptistry for the purpose.

A secret Protestant church

In contrast to the Catholics, the Protestants were not united in their beliefs and various denominations arose, each with its own church or chapel. However, the dissenters, as they were called, hardly ever received official permission to build their own place of worship. One such group, the Mennonites, built a chapel (called *Vermaning*, from the Dutch word to exhort or to admonish) in Workum, Friesland (above right). Its location is typical of chapels belonging to communities which did not follow the official line; in this case in an enclosed yard, behind the sexton's house. It looks like a barn from the outside and was built in 1694 in a very simple style in accordance with Mennonite beliefs.

Print showing the Oostkerk, Middelburg (1746).

Left: The Mennonite Chapel, Workum, Friesland (1694).

Below: Protestant service in the Nieuwe Zijds Kapel about 1655. Painting in the Catharijne convent Museum, Utrecht.

Synagogues

Of course the Jewish community has always had its own places of worship and the largest number of synagogues in the Netherlands was in Amsterdam. The Portuguese Synagogue (below), consecrated in 1675, is one of the few still standing. Its height, which would have been more obvious in the 17th century when houses were smaller, is in keeping with Jewish law which lays down that a synagogue must be taller than the surrounding buildings.
The row of small houses around it is to accommodate the various official rooms such as living quarters, the ritual bath and rooms for teaching.

Columns divide the synagogue into three tunnel-vaulted bays.
The women's galleries are situated in the aisles since the sexes were strictly segregated during worship.
On the eastern side is the ark containing the Torah, the five books of Moses in the form of a scroll.
On the opposite side is the 'Bimah' or dais from which the readings from the Torah are given.
The seats are arranged on either side of the aisle between the ark and the 'Bimah'.

The Portugese Synagogue, Amsterdam (1675).

Nieuwe Kerk, Amsterdam, pulpit.

Nieuwe Kerk, Amsterdam, pulpit (detail).

Roman Catholic Church of Our Lady, Asten.

The eighteenth century

Few new churches were built in the 18th century, for two reasons: the Protestants had enough churches, partly because they had taken over so many during the Reformation, and obstacles were put in the way of 'unofficial' denominations.

The nineteenth century

In accordance with ideas reaching the Netherlands from Revolutionary France, the privileged position of the Dutch Reformed Church was abolished in 1795 and every denomination was given the right to build its own churches.
The majority of the churches built in the 19th century were Catholic, as the Protestants retained possession of the churches they had taken over during the Reformation, except in the province of North Brabant.

SS Mary and Brigid, Geldrop; interior.

Neo-classicism

Neo-classicism, the predominant style of the first half of the 19th century, was inspired by the architecture of ancient Greece and Rome.
A good example of this style is the Church of St. Petrus Banden (St. Peter in Chains) in Driebergen-Rijsenburg (page 94). The columns and pediment around the entrance are reminiscent of the façade of a Greek temple, while the semi-circular forecourt makes one think of the famous 17th-century semi-circular colonnade in front of St. Peter's in Rome.

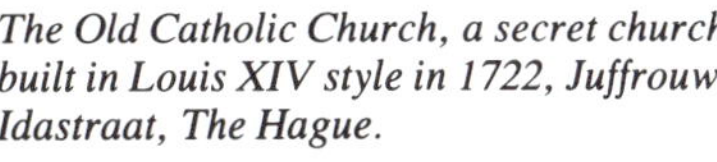

The Old Catholic Church, a secret church built in Louis XIV style in 1722, Juffrouw Idastraat, The Hague.

Basilica, Oudenbosch (North Brabant).

Early 19th century Church of St. Petrus' Banden (St. Peter in chains), Driebergen-Rijsenburg. Photograph taken early this century by B. Kraal.

The Gothic revival

As its name implies, this 19th-century style was inspired by the Gothic architecture of the Middle Ages, notably the 13th-century French cathedrals which aroused great admiration and interest.

One of the most famous Dutch architects of the Gothic revival was P. J. H. Cuypers who took the photograph shown on the opposite page of St. Catherine's Church in Eindhoven which he also designed. It is an expression of 19th-century creativity which aims at breathing fresh life into mediaeval architecture, rather than a copy of a French cathedral.

The Gothic revival was interested in both the form and the symbolism of mediaeval architecture; the sturdy right-hand tower of St. Catherine's with its lookout post and battlements represents the tower of David.

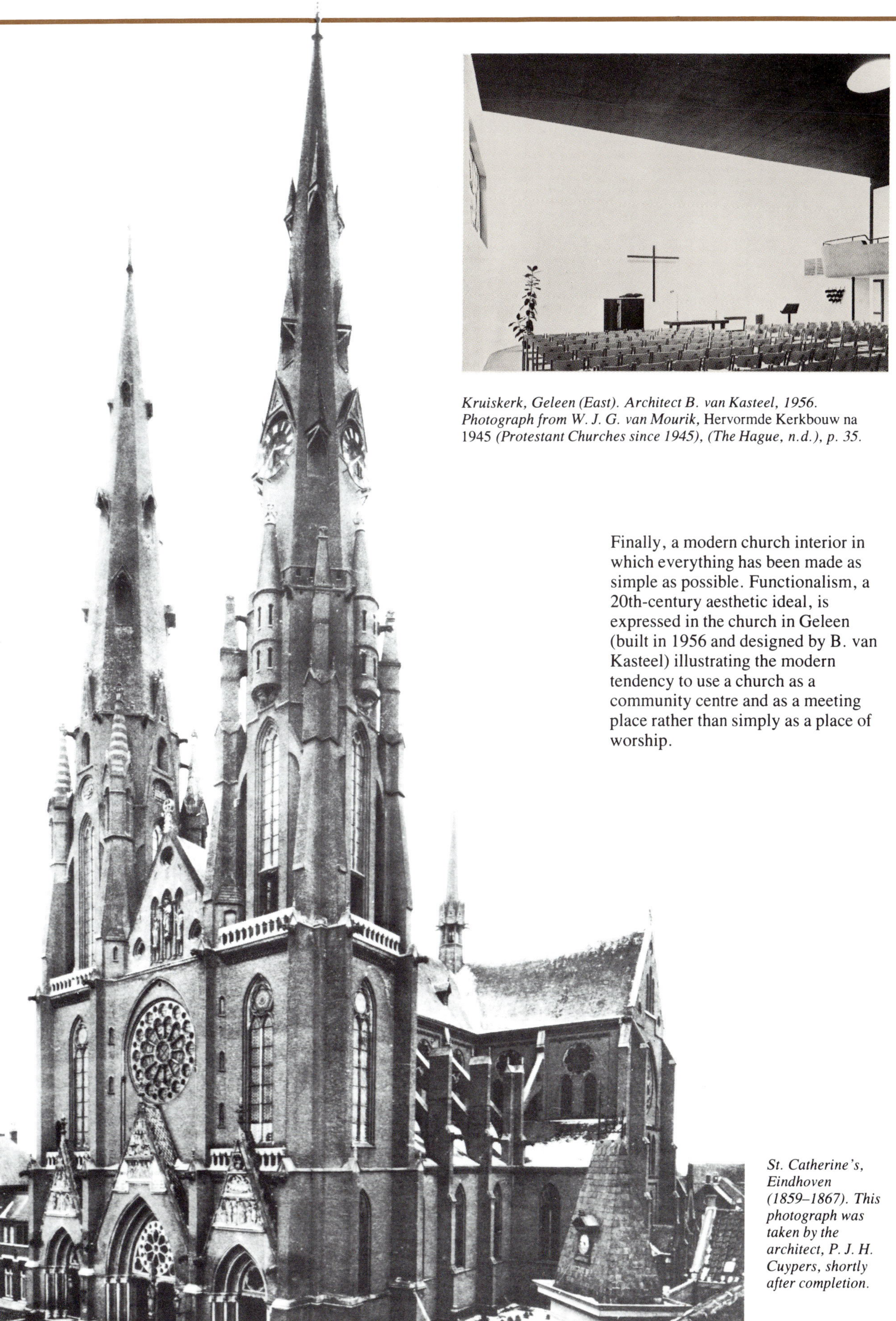

Kruiskerk, Geleen (East). Architect B. van Kasteel, 1956. Photograph from W. J. G. van Mourik, Hervormde Kerkbouw na 1945 *(Protestant Churches since 1945), (The Hague, n.d.), p. 35.*

Finally, a modern church interior in which everything has been made as simple as possible. Functionalism, a 20th-century aesthetic ideal, is expressed in the church in Geleen (built in 1956 and designed by B. van Kasteel) illustrating the modern tendency to use a church as a community centre and as a meeting place rather than simply as a place of worship.

St. Catherine's, Eindhoven (1859–1867). This photograph was taken by the architect, P. J. H. Cuypers, shortly after completion.

Farmhouses

Farmhouses... historic buildings. In Holland, farmhouses are an integral part of the landscape. In fact it would be difficult to imagine the flat Dutch countryside without them.

A number of old farmhouses have been designated as historic buildings under the Monuments and Historic Buildings Act, because they are 'more than 50 years old and are worth preserving because of their beauty, or their scientific or ethnological importance'.

Old farmhouses come in all shapes and sizes; some of the most common types are described here.

Most people think of a farm as a place in the country with cows, chickens and sometimes even horses, although nowadays almost all the latter have been replaced by machines.

But few people know how farmhouses were actually built and what materials were used – the subject of this chapter.

Several factors influenced the design of the farmhouse: one was whether it was to be an arable farm, a dairy farm or a mixed farm.
Another was the fact that people preferred to use those building materials such as wood, stone, reed or clay, which were to be found in the vicinity of the site. Naturally the actual structure of the building was also important and here, too, there were several variations (see pages 106-113).
Finally, the type of soil on which the farmhouse was to be built had to be taken in account. It is therefore not surprising that there are so many kinds of farmhouses in the Netherlands.
In fact Dutch farmhouses can be divided into several 'families' or groups which can themselves be divided into different categories.
The Frisian house group is to be found in part of North Holland, in the provinces of Friesland, Groningen and the Frisian Islands.
By far the largest 'family', the *Halle house group,* is to be found in the provinces of Drente, Overijssel, Gelderland, Utrecht and South Holland, and in the Gooi area.
In Limburg and a part of North Brabant the *Limburg group* can be seen.
Farmhouses belonging to the *Zeeland barn group* can be seen in Zeeland and those belonging to the *Flemish barn group* are found in North Brabant.

Hummelo (Gelderland).

All of the above are shown in the photographs and their most important features are described.

Frisian House Group

Farmhouse with pyramid roof ('stolp' farmhouse)
This type, typical of North Holland, is square and simple in plan: a square hayrick in the centre is marked off by four massive wooden posts and is surrounded by the living and working areas.
The roof is in the shape of a pyramid and is usually covered with a combination of black, glazed tiles and thatch which together form a pattern. The tiled area is called the farmhouse's 'mirror'.
The front of the farmhouse, which is built out to one side of the square, looks just like an ordinary house.
The farm is surrounded by trees, which shade it from the sun when they are in leaf and also protect it against storms.

Hoogwoud (North Holland).

'Stelp' farmhouse
The 'stelp' type of farm is common in the south-west corner of Friesland and is extremely well-suited to cattle farming. It resembles the pyramid farmhouse of North Holland but is rectangular rather than square in plan and therefore has more room to store hay. The rectangular construction also means that the roof is not pointed but has a long ridge.

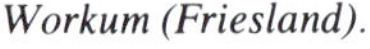

Workum (Friesland).

Finsterwolde (Groningen).

Oldamster type
Groningen boasts an impressive type of farm, adapted for arable farming, named after the place of its origin, the Oldambt.
The broad living area and the barn are built one behind the other under one long roof.
A series of steps in the outside walls show how the living-area gradually widens towards the back of the house and eventually becomes the barn.
A feature of these farmhouses is that they have one or more lofts above the living quarters where grain can be stored. The loft can be recognized from the outside by its small, rectangular windows.
The living area sometimes resembles a townhouse.

'Head, neck and body' type
This type is found in Friesland and many parts of Groningen and usually belongs to a mixed arable and dairy farm.
The 'head' is the farmhouse itself under which there is a milk cellar, the 'neck' consists of the domestic working area, and the 'body' is the barn where there are stalls for cows and horses, mows for grain and hay and a threshing floor. The gable ends of the barn area are often decorated (see photograph) with a triangular apex called an 'oelebord'.

Boxum (Friesland).

Denekamp (Overijssel).

Halle house group

This is still the most widespread group in the Netherlands although here too, there are regional differences. All of these farmhouses, however, have the following features:

- an anchor-beam frame (consisting of two stout posts joined by a tie-beam which is 'anchored' on the outside by wooden pegs; see also page 106);
- a triple aisled structure (consisting of an aisle on either side of a central nave);
- a covered hayrick instead of a barn.

The Halle house type of farm developed from the 'losse hoes', a large open building with no partition between the living quarters and the barn. Unfortunately, as a result of storms, fires and modernization, there are very few examples of this type left, though at one time they were to be found extensively in Drente, Twente and the Achterhoek.

Twente half-timbered farmhouse
Half-timbered walls are a striking feature of the Twente farmhouse. The building has an oak frame filled in with wattle and daub and sometimes finished off with hand-made, pale-red bricks.
The wooden gable ends were often painted with a special sort of paint known as 'ox blood', the colour of which goes very well with the red brick.

Drente farmhouse
In the course of time, a dividing wall was built in the 'losse hoes' between the living quarters and the barn which remained one building.
The large barn doors at the back and sides are recessed slightly to make them high enough to take fully-laden hay carts. The roofs are nearly always thatched.
In this example the farmhouses are grouped informally, and make a charming picture of a typical Drente community.

Rouveen (Overijssel).

Staphorst and Rouveen farmhouse
The Halle house farmhouses in Staphorst and Rouveen constitute a separate type, found solely in these two villages.
Here, too, the living area is separated from the barn.
The former is usually built of brick, whereas the barn, which has doors opening to the threshing floor in the side wall, is of wood. The whole structure is covered by one large thatched roof. *Wooden* chimneys are also a characteristic feature. The doors and shutters are painted bright blue.

'Krukhuis' type
There are many large cheese farms in the low-lying districts of South Holland to the west of the Hollandse IJssel. The 'krukhuis' – literally 'crutch house' – type of farmhouse gets its name from its L-shaped plan; the living area is built out to one side and thus is broader than the stalls behind. A milk cellar and a storage place for cheese have been accommodated under a part of the ground floor.
The painted crucifixes above the cellar windows were, according to tradition, supposed to ward off the 'evil eye' of spirits which could turn the milk.

Hoogmade (South Holland).

Tuil (Gelderland).

Bergambacht (South Holland).

T-shaped farmhouses
The living quarters of the type of Halle house found in Gelderland, eastern Utrecht and the Yssel district have been extended on both sides to form a T-shaped building. The living area is the bar of the T, as can be seen in the photograph.

Polsbroek (Utrecht).

Farmhouses in the Lopikerwaard, Krimpenerwaard and Alblasserwaard

Farmhouses in the above districts, like this one in Polsbroek in the Province of Utrecht, also belong to the Halle house 'family'. High water levels had to be taken into account when building. Floors were built higher than usual in the hope that the interior would remain dry in the event of flooding. As a result the windows and the front door, which is approached by means of 'flood steps', are high up in the wall.

Farmhouse in Bergambacht

The doors and windows of this farmhouse in Bergambacht in the Krimpenerwaard are also above ground level. The living quarters are at right angles to the barn and the result is a T-shaped plan. The gables, especially those at the side, the ornamental cramp irons, the wrought iron on the chimneys and the attractive brickwork all give the building a rather grand appearance.

Limburg group

In this group the living and working quarters are side by side and the entrances are positioned along the front.
Such farmhouses are to be found in parts of North Brabant and Limburg.

Schimmert (Limburg).

Chaam (North Brabant).

The 'Long roof' type
This simple type of farmhouse was built on the sandy soil of North Brabant. The living quarters, stalls and barn lie alongside each other under one roof and the doors and windows open on to the road.

Raren (Limburg).

Atrium farmhouse
Atrium farmhouses are to be found in the south of Limburg: originally L-shaped in plan, they later became U-shaped. The large doorway from the street leads to a yard around which the living quarters and barns are grouped. The example shown is in Schimmert; it is built of marlstone from Limburg quarries and crowned with a particularly beautiful gable. The living quarters are also strikingly similar to an ordinary townhouse. Farmhouses near the River Maas are usually white-washed. The window-frames and door-frames are of stone – another common feature of townhouses in south Limburg.

South Limburg half-timbered farmhouse
Groups of half-timbered farm buildings are to be found in the south of Limburg. The outside walls are constructed from an oak frame filled in with wattle and daub. The picture shows the wooden frame before it is filled in (right), the finished white-washed walls (just visible in the centre) and finally the finished walls with tarred oak beams.

Zeeland and Flemish barn group

Borssele (Zeeland).

Zeeland barn
The barn is the largest and most important part of this type of farmhouse, the house being much smaller. The latter was built of brick and covered with roof-tiles, whereas the enormous barn was constructed of black-tarred wood and often covered with a thatched roof raised slightly in places to accommodate large doors. The barns are usually of the Limburg type: their main doors are situated in the long side wall. Window-frames and door-frames are picked out in white. The smaller door in the barn door allows easy access to the barn itself.

Farmhouse construction

Old farmhouses were built to satisfy a number of requirements and contained living quarters for people and animals, storage space for hay and corn, room for equipment (carts, ploughs etc.) and such work as threshing, churning and baking.

Diagram of a wooden frame with anchor-beams.

Farmhouse roofs may rest on a wooden frame, stone walls or a combination of both.
The wooden frame consists of a number of cross-beams placed one behind the other and connected by means of wall plates along the top on which the actual roof rests.
There are two types of frame, the anchor-beam frame and the deck-beam frame, both of which consist of posts (vertical supports), horizontal beams (the anchor or deck-beams) and two corbels (diagonal beams between the posts and the horizontal beams).

Dinteloord (North Brabant).

Flemish barn

The Dinteloord farmhouse shown here is typical of the type built on the sea-clay soil of north-west Brabant. At first sight the barn looks like that of the Zeeland type, but it is different in that it has a passage running from front to back. For this reason the doors are situated in the shorter wall. The house itself is somewhat larger than that of the Zeeland type. The extra height is due to the loft (which sometimes consists of two storeys) where grain is stored.

An *anchor-beam* has tenons at each end which fit into mortices in the posts and are anchored by wooden pegs where they protrude at the sides. The wall plates rest on the posts. (See photograph and diagram on page 108.)

A *deck-beam* lies across the top of the posts, and is secured by means of a tenon on the post which fits into a mortice in the beam. The wall plates rest on the ends of the deck beams. (See photograph and diagram on page 110.)

The wall plates support rafters to which planks are nailed which in turn carry the roofing (usually thatch or tiles).

Sometimes (especially in south Limburg) the posts are incorporated into the side wall but usually they stand clear of the walls inside the building, in which case they divide the interior into three areas, a high central nave and two low aisles at each side.

Deck-beam frames are most common in many parts of Groningen, Friesland and North Holland, the north-west of Overyssel and Zeeland. *Anchor-beam frames* are less common in the above provinces but are found in all others.

There are also variations on these two basic types: sometimes the tenons on the anchor-beams do not stick through the posts, or else the entire beam sticks through the post. The latter variation is found in the east and south-east but it is only possible if the beams are placed high up in the posts. Deck-beams can extend over one or both posts and there are also frames with two horizontal beams.

Roofs resting solely on *stone* or *brick walls* are especially common in Limburg. The weight of the roof is distributed by means of roof trusses over wooden beams positioned on or in the walls. (See photograph and diagram on page 113.)

Farm with anchor-beam frame

A farmhouse near Barneveld of the Halle house type illustrates the anchor-beam type of construction. The plan of the farmhouse and a cross section of the barn are shown here. The living quarters and the barn are housed under one roof which is supported by seven anchor-beams. The living quarters and the barn are divided by a partition.

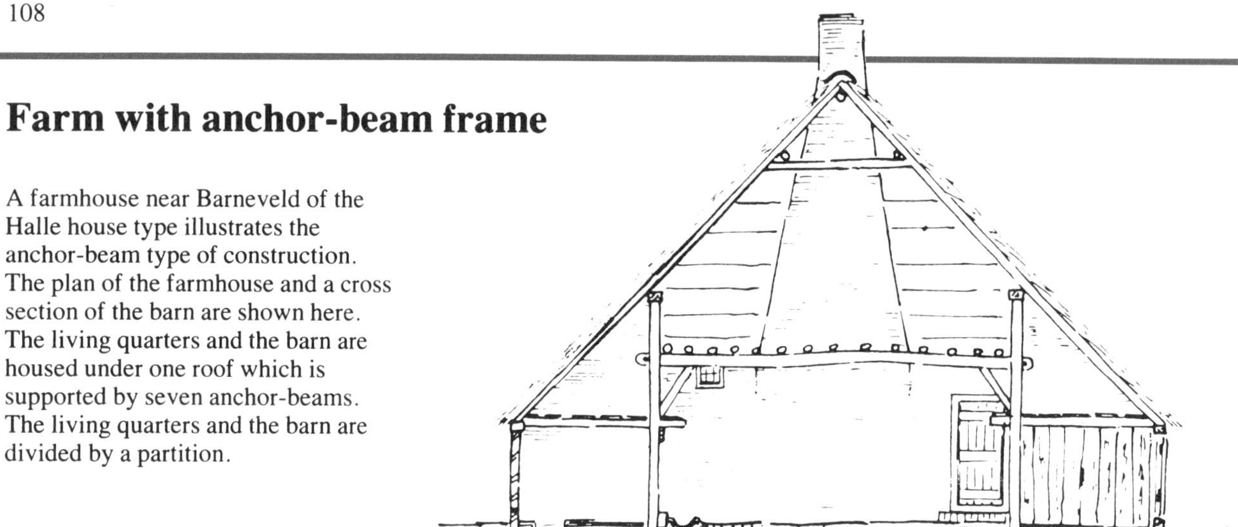

cross section A-B

Barn in the 'De Clef' farmhouse in Ewijk, Gelderland: wood-frame construction with anchor-beams.

The nave of the barn constitutes the threshing floor. The harvest is stored above this on top of thin tree trunks placed across the anchor-beams. The aisle on the right is the cowstall; the other aisle contains a stable and storage space. There is also room for storing the harvest above the aisles.

The living quarters consist of a large kitchen in the centre with rooms (such as the dairy) on either side. The fire-place stands against the dividing wall and has a hood and chimney above it to extract the smoke. By placing a cupboard bed next to the warm hearth the occupants kept themselves warm in winter.

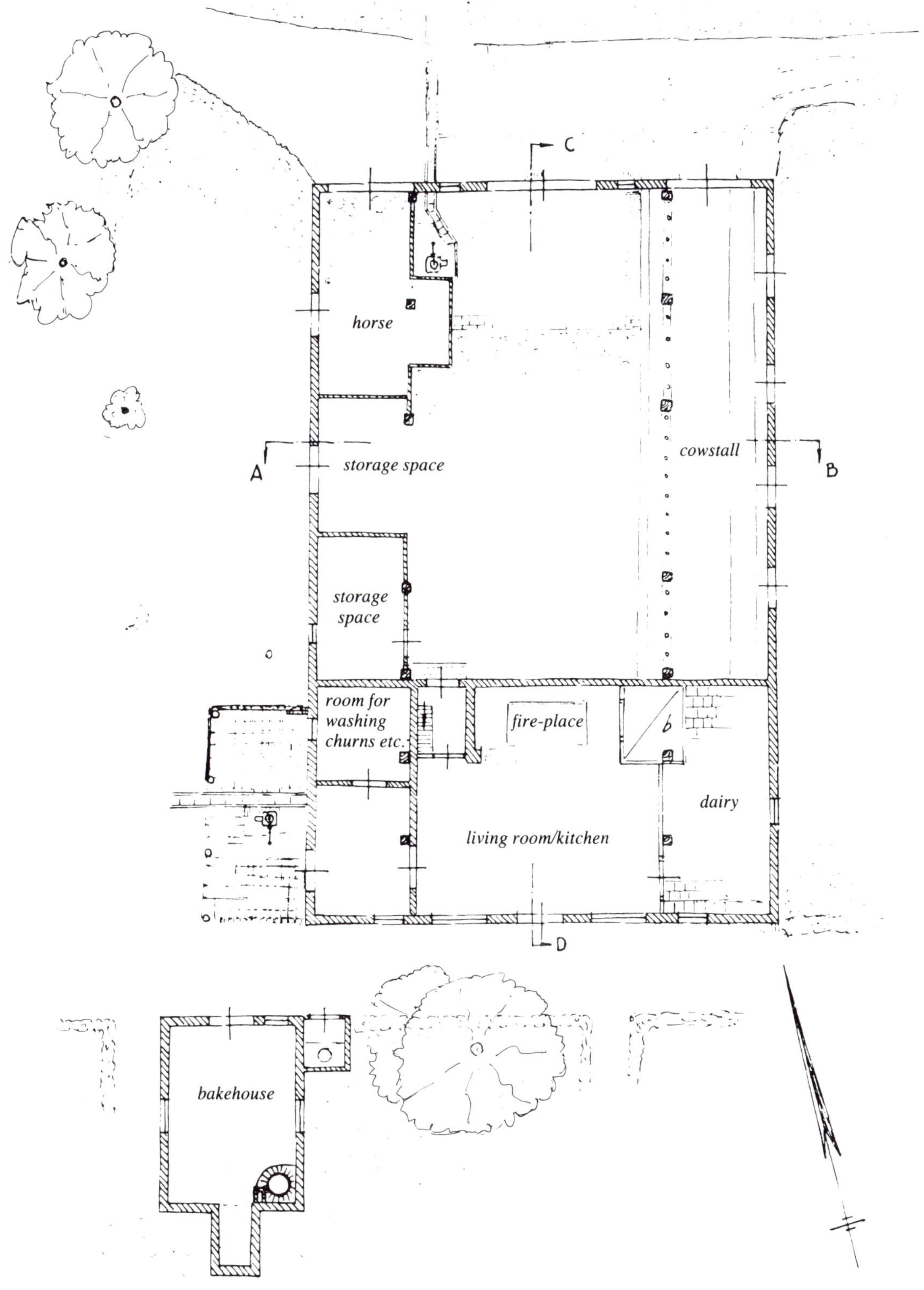

Farm with deck-beam frame

Remains of a demolished farmhouse near Avenhorn (North Holland) showing roof trusses.

This 'head, neck and body' type of farmhouse situated near Bedum in the province of Groningen was constructed with deck-beams and is shown here in plan and cross section. The large roof is supported by six deck-beam frames and the low sidewalls.

Most of the central nave is used as a haymow. One of the aisles accommodates the cow stalls and a room extending outwards slightly for a farm labourer. The other aisle is the threshing floor where the hay carts entered with the harvest.

The living quarters are in the 'head' of the farmhouse and next to them is a somewhat sunken cellar under the sloping roof.

The 'neck' houses the kitchen and churning room which provides access to two storage rooms, the cellar and the dairy in the low section at the front of the barn.

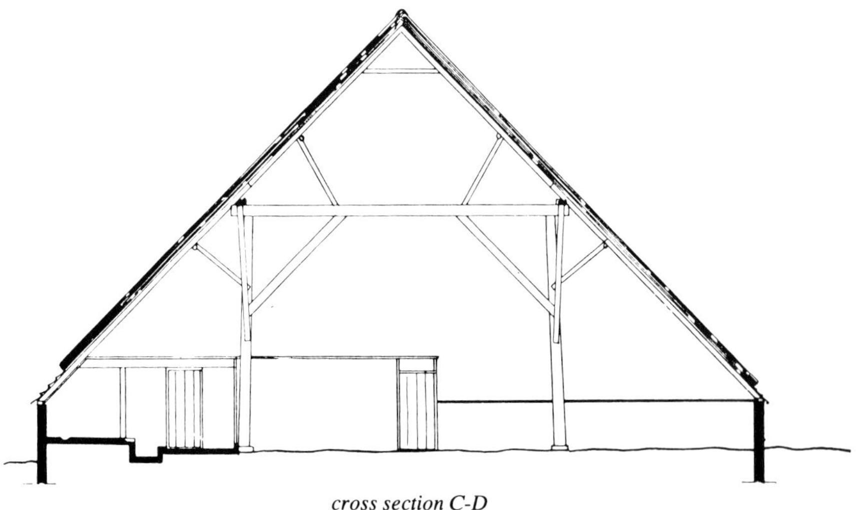

cross section C-D

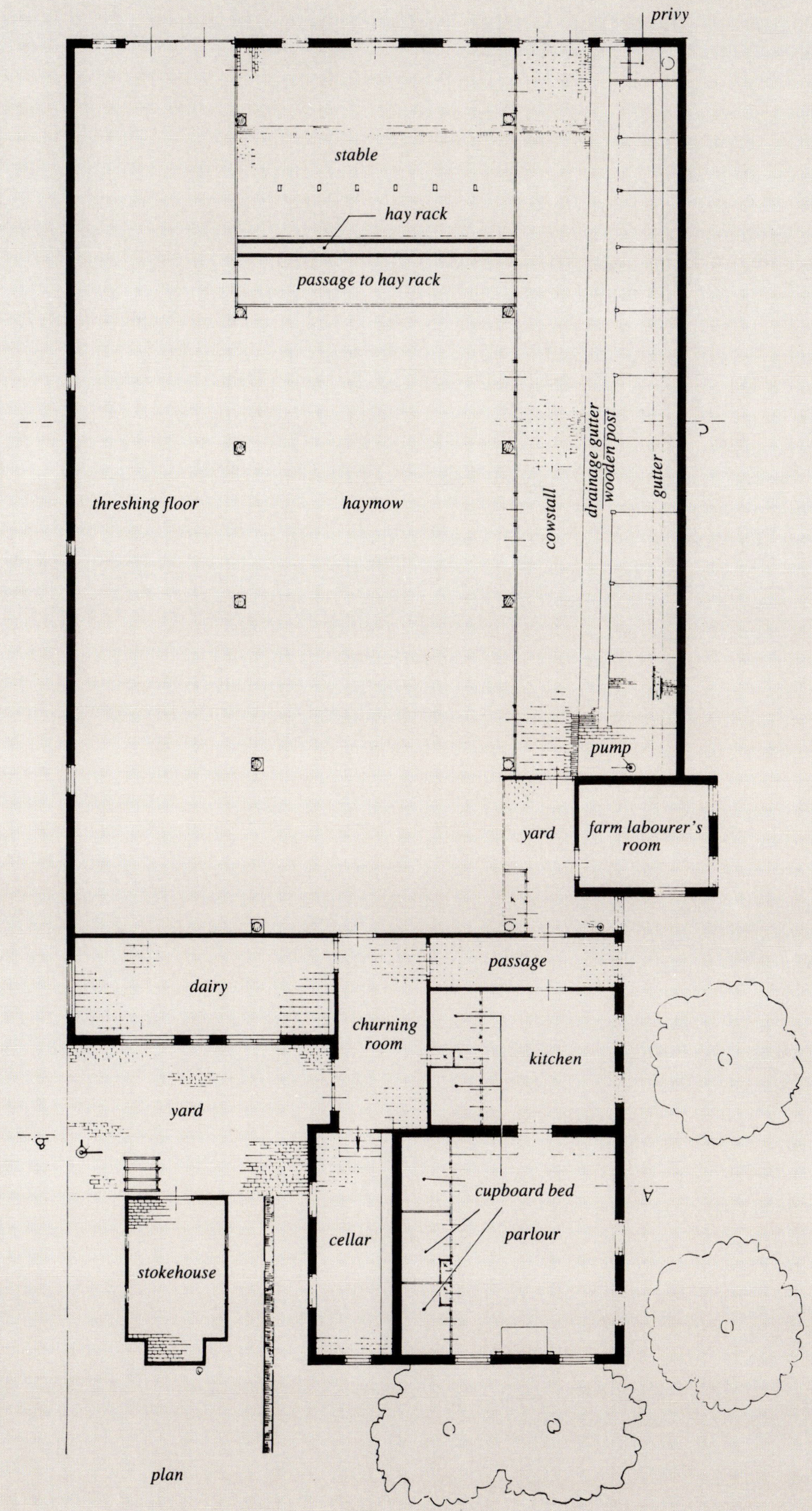
privy
stable
hay rack
passage to hay rack
threshing floor
haymow
cowstall
drainage gutter
wooden post
gutter
pump
yard
farm labourer's room
passage
dairy
churning room
kitchen
yard
cupboard bed
parlour
cellar
stokehouse
A
A
plan

Farmhouse with stone supporting walls

Granary of the Puth manor-house near Voerendaal (South Limburg); the roof is supported by brick walls.

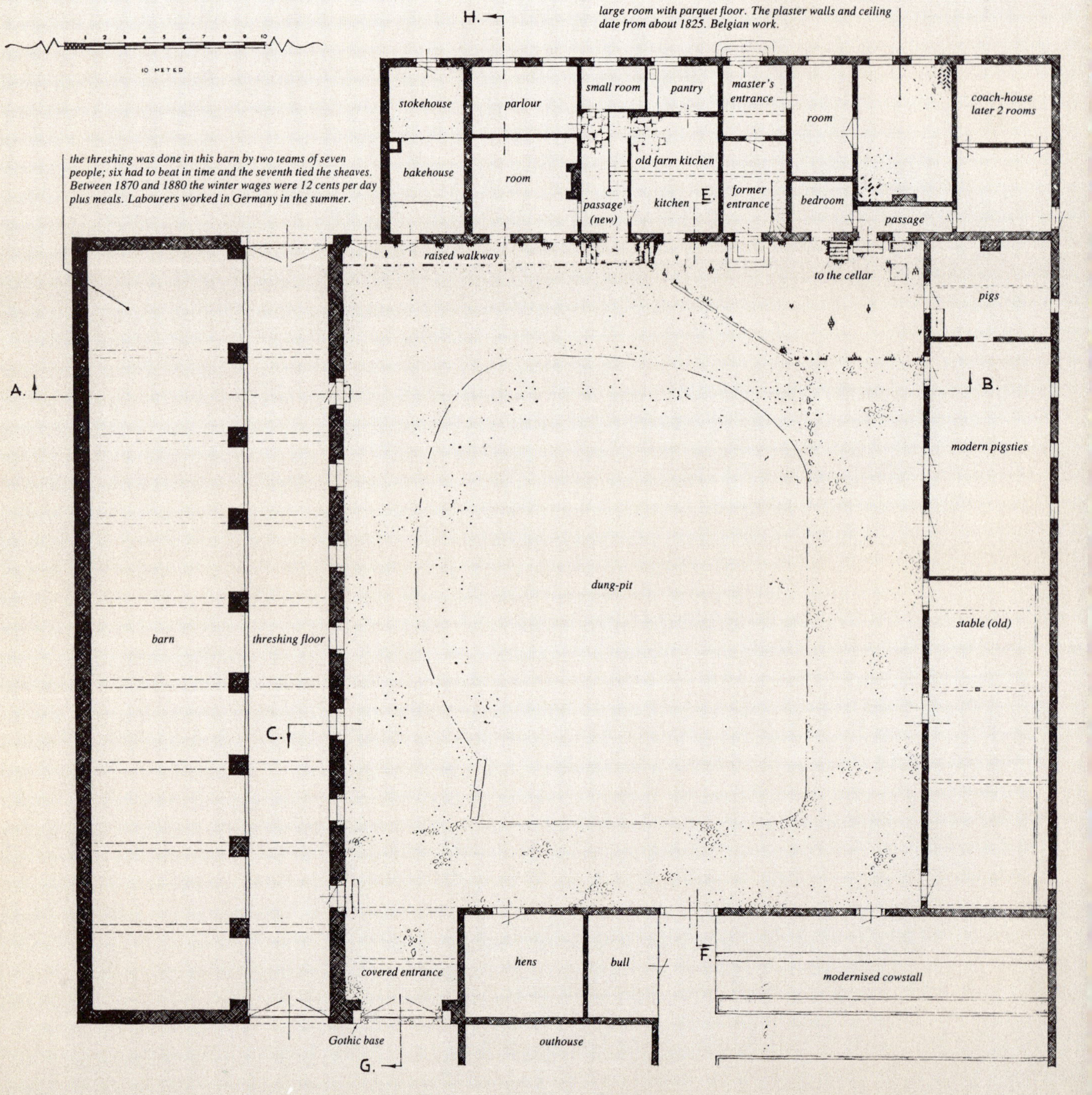

H.

large room with parquet floor. The plaster walls and ceiling date from about 1825. Belgian work.

1 2 3 4 5 6 7 8 9 10

10 METER

stokehouse

parlour

small room

pantry

master's entrance

room

coach-house later 2 rooms

the threshing was done in this barn by two teams of seven people; six had to beat in time and the seventh tied the sheaves. Between 1870 and 1880 the winter wages were 12 cents per day plus meals. Labourers worked in Germany in the summer.

bakehouse

room

old farm kitchen

passage (new)

kitchen

E.

former entrance

bedroom

passage

raised walkway

to the cellar

pigs

A.

B.

modern pigsties

dung-pit

barn

threshing floor

stable (old)

C.

F.

hens

bull

covered entrance

modernised cowstall

Gothic base

outhouse

G.

plan

An atrium farmhouse near Geleen in south Limburg illustrates this type. The various activities which are carried out on the farm take place in the long buildings situated around the yard. One of the four sections houses the living quarters and two others provide accommodation for animals. The fourth serves as a barn for storing hay and for threshing.
The framework consists of stone walls, on top of which are beams and roof trusses, which support the roof. The barn has two aisles as each beam is supported by a brick pillar. There is a midden in the centre of the yard, which can be entered through an opening in one of the sides.

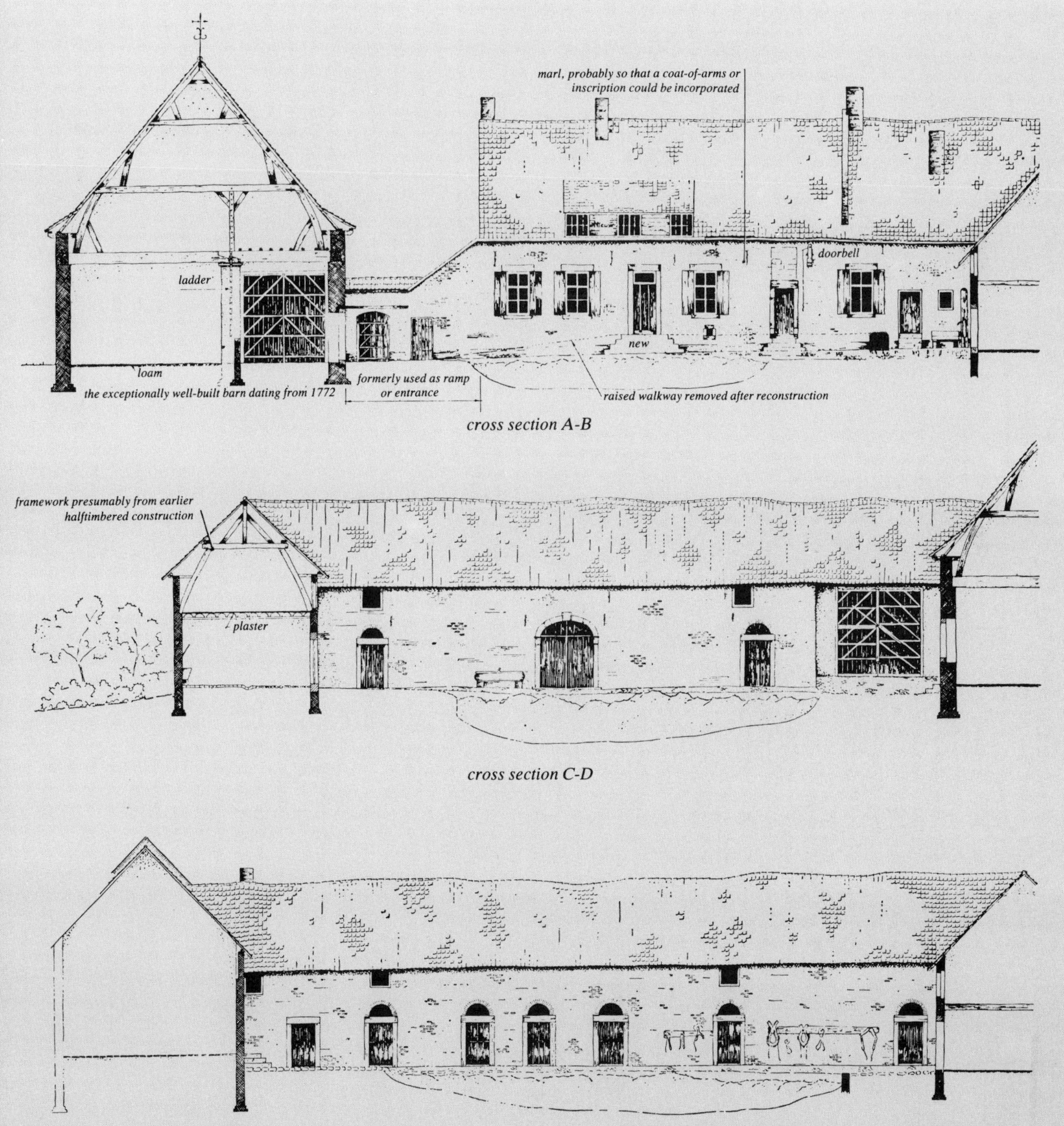

cross section A-B

cross section C-D

cross section E-F

Windmills

A flat landscape, dikes, grass swaying in the breeze, large stretches of water and windmills; all this is instantly recognizable as a typical Dutch scene, especially the windmills.

Not so very long ago mills were essential to the Dutch economy; they ground corn, processed cocoa, dyewood and chalk, hulled barley, sawed wood and made paper. They also played an important role in shaping the Dutch landscape: they were used to pump lakes dry and create fertile, agricultural 'polders', as the areas of reclaimed land are called. They are still used nowadays to keep the water level in the polders under control. It would be fair to say that without them, the low-lying parts of the Netherlands as we know them today would never have existed.

Left: Paltrok sawmill (foreground) and octagonal paint mill with platform. Zaandam (North Holland).

The corn-mill grinds and the miller examines the quality of the flour.

Octagonal corn and hulling mill with platform, Westerwijtwerd (Groningen).

It is not known for certain when the first mills came into being, but there is no doubt that before the year 1000, watermills, driven by rivers and streams, were grinding corn in the higher-lying areas of the Netherlands – long before the first windmills.
By 1274 windmills were evidently a more familiar sight, as mention is made of them in a charter presented by Count Floris V to the burghers of Haarlem. A text dating from 1294 refers to post mills used for grinding corn in Lochem and five years later to similar mills in St. Oedenrode. The earliest known drainage mills date from 1414, and they were found in many parts of the province of South Holland after 1450.
The accompanying photographs show some of the many different types of windmills.
The post mill, the oldest type, consists of a mill-house and sails built around a vertical shaft or post, all of which can be turned to catch the wind.
The *hollow post mill* looks like the post mill but is not as high and the house is cubelike.
Another type, the *tower mill*, was usually built of brick.
Drainage mills can be either octagonal and wooden or round and made of brick; the majority are 'cap winders' which can be turned into the wind or 'winded' by means of a winch or handwheel on the outside, as opposed to the less elegant inside winders.
Platform mills, as the name suggests, have a platform to enable the miller to tend to the sails.
'Ground-sail' mills have sails which barely skim the ground and finally the *'mill in a mound'* type is built in or on a mound of earth.
There are also different types of *watermill*.

Information on all of the above can be obtained from the Educatieve Dienst van het Nederlands Openlucht-museum (The Education Service of the Netherlands Open Air Museum), Schelmseweg 89, Arnhem.

Octagonal drainage mill, 't Waar (Groningen).

Octagonal drainage mill ('monk mill'), Workum (Friesland).

'He's got windmills in his head'

(Dutch saying – He's out of his mind)

'Spider mill' (drainage mill), Wirdum (Friesland).

The mills not used for pumping water served as water or wind-driven grinding machines. Their machinery, usually wooden, was built centuries ago by skilled craftsmen, using all their knowledge and experience of architecture, mechanical and hydraulic engineering and aerodynamics. The result was efficient machinery which has subsequently served many generations. Mills were built to accommodate axles, cog-wheels and milling stones and are therefore often unsuitable for habitation.
As a result whole-scale renovation is taking place, involving repairing the machinery in the 'heart' of the mill and the structure of the actual building.
In fact only about fifty wind and water mills still do a job of work.
Nowadays however there is great interest in preservation and on certain days the sails of an increasing number of unused mills are rotated by enthusiasts.
For another thing, people now want flour ground by the traditional method, which has the added attraction that it does not cause air or water pollution. In this way more and more mills are being given a new lease of life, adding an attracting feature to many towns and villages as well as keeping the miller's craft alive at the same time.

Octagonal corn mill with platform, Norg (Drenthe).

'The miller is kind to his donkey as long as it carries his sacks of corn'

(Dutch proverb)

Octagonal mill with platform, Olst (Overijssel).

Octagonal corn mill with platform, Sloten (Friesland).

Tower mill (corn mill), Zeddam (Gelderland).

Octagonal corn mill with platform, Klarenbeek (Gelderland).

Water mill, Haaksbergen (Overijssel). Formerly oil and corn mill.

Water mill (corn mill), Eibergen (Gelderland).

'My mill won't grind any more'

(I can't chew anything)

There used to be literally thousands of mills in the Netherlands – a century ago there were 11,000 – but by 1900 the number had dropped to 2,500. Now the figure stands at less than one thousand. They were sacrificed in the name of progress once they had apparently outlived their usefulness. Many mills fell into disuse with the advent of steam engines, and, subsequently, diesel engines and electrically-powered machinery, all of

Below: Octagonal corn mill with platform, Oudorp (North Holland).

Below right: Octanogal saw mill with platform, Leiden (South Holland).

Hollow post mill (drainage mill), Kockengen (Utrecht).

Octagonal drainage mill, Spanbroek (North Holland).

which were much more efficient.
The mills were taken off active service and then sorely neglected in their old age. Before long they stood out like sore thumbs until they were eventually demolished.
Every effort is now being made to preserve the mills which have survived, whatever the cost. And the cost cannot be overlooked – it is not unusual for renovation to come to more than 150,000 guilders!

A number of societies are concerned with the preservation of historic Dutch mills. In addition, the Department for the Preservation of Monuments and Historic Buildings has an annual budget of approximately one million guilders to spend on the renovation and maintenance of mills. The provinces and the municipalities provide more or less the same amount every year. Private organizations, which between them own 125 mills, also make funds available. There are nearly forty millwrights in the Netherlands, employing about a hundred craftsmen and they, too, are actively engaged in keeping the mills turning.

Octagonal drainage mill in series to raise water, Zevenhuizen (South Holland).

Hollow post mill (drainage mill), near Nieuwpoort (South Holland).

Round ground-sail corn mill, Colijnsplaat (Zeeland).

Open post mills (corn mills), Heusden (North Brabant).

Open post mill (corn mill), Kruiningen (Zeeland).

Round corn mills with platforms, Wemeldinge (Zeeland).

Round corn mill in a mound, Luyksgestel (North Brabant).

The windmill is practically the national emblem of Holland, probably because there are so many of them: their large frames dominate the flat polders, towering above buildings in towns and villages. In days gone by, they often acted as beacons or landmarks. But times have changed: urban expansion, sky-scrapers, new roads and drastic changes in water control have all led to the demise of these elegant structures from a bygone age.

Mills have become surrounded by other buildings or overgrown by vegetation, so that sometimes it is even difficult to find them. They become cut off from the wind or the water, pushed aside, as it were, serving no useful purpose. It goes without saying that they deserve better treatment and that measures must be taken to ensure that they get it. Preserving windmills means preserving the open countryside around them, thereby enabling them to continue to operate. It is of the utmost importance that the remaining 1030 mills should be kept in working condition – in hard times they could even guarantee a supply of food and protect the polders from flooding.

Water mill (corn mill and formerly oil and saw mill), Opwetten (North Brabant).

Water mill (corn mill), Wijlre (Limburg).

Corn mill in a mound, Roggel (Limburg).

Half-closed post mill (corn mill), Baexem (Limburg).

The miller

Being a miller was often a family tradition; the tricks of the trade were passed on from father to son. A miller could tell by looking at the sky what the wind was going to do. If his predictions were inaccurate, the weather with all its whims and fancies, could cause untold damage to his precious mill.

The only way to learn the miller's trade is by experience over many years. Before the mill can grind, the sails have to be turned into the wind and, depending on its force, be entirely or partly covered with cloth. Even then, the miller must still keep his eyes open for changes in the weather!

'He was once a bishop and now he's a miller'

(He's gone down in the world)

Mill renovation in Abcoude (Utrecht) in 1904. A new sail axel is being put in place.

The four hundred year old drainage mill in Alkmaar (North Holland).

The old drainage mill, 'De 1200 Roe', Amsterdam. It is no longer in use and has lost its function as a landmark.

Drainage mill in Streefkerk (South Holland) as it used to be and in its present state. The waterways around the mill have been filled in and the dykes levelled out, leaving the mill high and dry. It can never again be used for pumping water. Note the wilderness which has been allowed to grow around it.

Fixing the sail-cloths. Kockengen (Utrecht).

This mill in Schoorl (North Holland) has gradually become overgrown.

The mill is 'winded'. Rijpwetering (South Holland).

'An idle mill grinds no corn'

Drainage mill in Lieshout (North Brabant).

Two grinding mills, Schiedam (South Holland).

The 'Ooievaar' (Stork) windmill in Zaandam in festive mood. The mill was used for pressing oil from seeds.

The codes

Windmills had their own language which is sometimes still used. By changing the position of the sails, the miller could let people for miles around know of his joy or grief. The codes varied from district to district. For instance, in the Zaan district near Amsterdam, all the laths were removed from the sails when the miller died and the sails were turned to point towards the house. If the miller's wife died one lath was left, whereas two were left when a son or daughter died. A happy occasion, such as a wedding or birth, was reason to decorate the mill with pine branches and bunting, with perhaps a sun symbolizing luck and a cage symbolizing marriage. Everyone shared in the miller's lot. If his mill was going to be out of use for some time, because the millstones had to be sharpened, because there was no work, or because the mill had broken down, the miller also indicated this by the position of the sails.

Windmill in Rijpwetering (South Holland).

Millstones have to be sharpened from time to time, when worn channels are recarved.

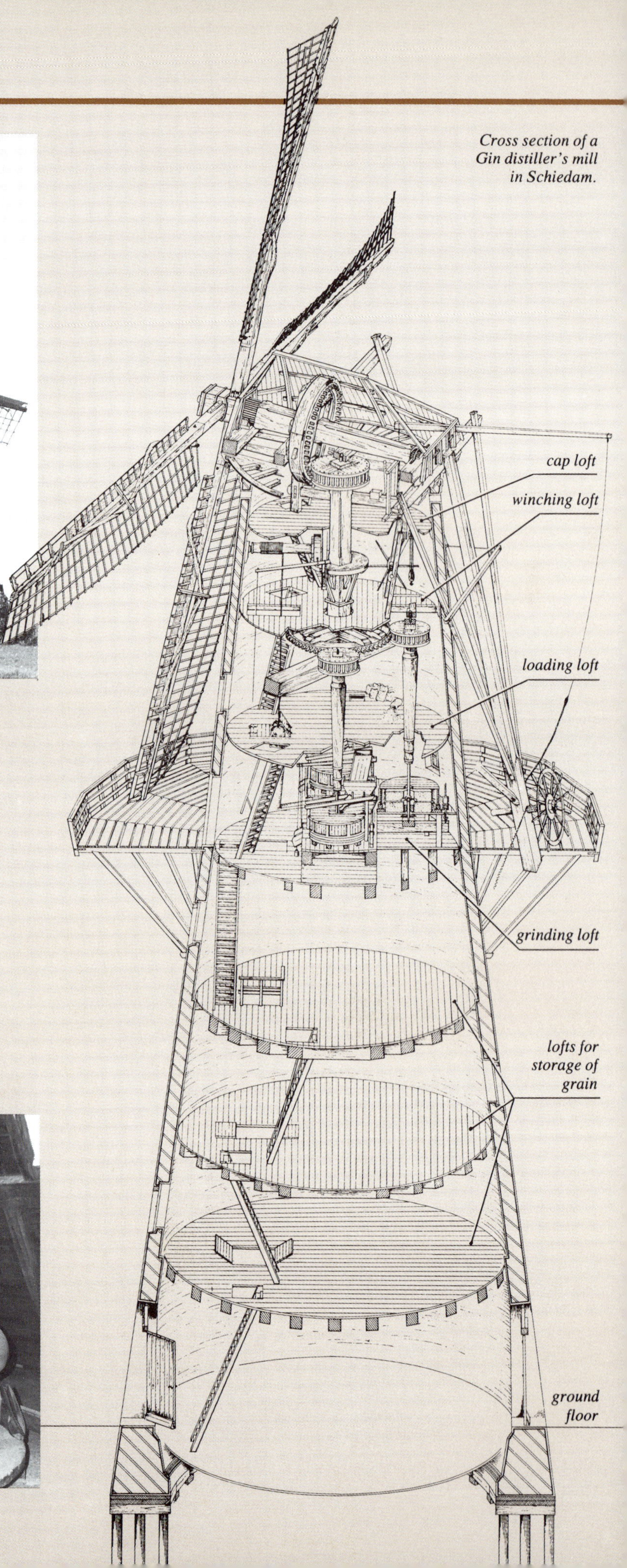

Cross section of a Gin distiller's mill in Schiedam.

cap loft

winching loft

loading loft

grinding loft

lofts for storage of grain

ground floor

The same tower mill before and after renovation, Grondsveld (Limburg).

A windmill in Valkenburg (South Holland) is given new sails in 1925.

The millwright

As windmills became important to the community, carpenters began to specialize in building and repairing them. The mills still standing today are the result of their know-how and experience. Mill construction was not something that could be learnt from books; in fact it was not until the first half of the 18th century that the first handbooks for millwrights appeared. All kinds of different types of wood were used, each of which was specially suited to a particular purpose.

The first millwrights did not have the powerful lifting equipment we use today, so they hoisted the heavy sections into place by means of derricks and capstans, hundreds of metres of thick rope and, above all, an incredible amount of muscle. Fortunately such operations can be carried out more easily and quickly nowadays during renovation.

Other monuments

The first six chapters in this book have described the most common types of monuments and historic buildings in the Netherlands.
This final chapter deals with buildings which are less obviously monuments but which nevertheless deserve to be considered as such because of their design or function.
We have chosen to present them in photographs since it would be impossible to describe them briefly. Perhaps in the future more space can be devoted to them in a sequel.

Foot-bridge, Edam (North Holland).

Steam pumping station, Medemblik (North Holland).

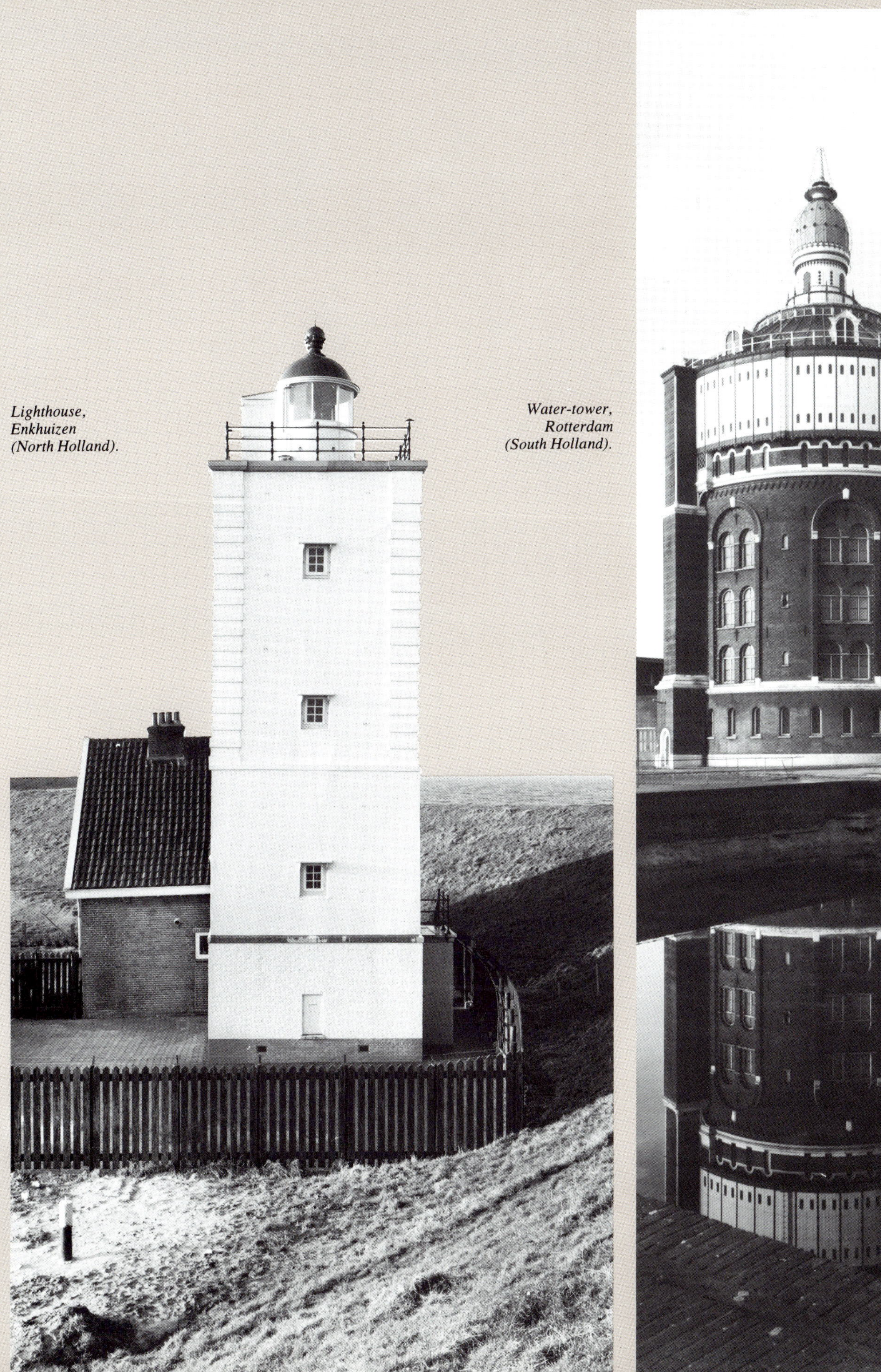

Lighthouse, Enkhuizen (North Holland).

Water-tower, Rotterdam (South Holland).

East gate, Delft (South Holland).

Pump, Noordwijk (South Holland).

East gate, Hoorn (North Holland).

Summer house, Baambrugge (Utrecht).

Central Station, Amsterdam (North Holland).

Railway Stations

Many of us take railway stations for granted – they are such an essential part of everyday life that it seems if they have always been there. By means of the rail network we travel from one town or village to another with the greatest of ease. Yet it was only relatively recently – in 1839 – that the first train came into operation in the Netherlands, between Amsterdam and Haarlem.
Unfortunately the only station which has survived from the early days of the railways is the one at Valkenburg, which resembles a castle and was built in 1853.
Large-scale expansion of the railways took place after 1860, some of which, including the building of stations, was undertaken by the State. The railways were, however, originally run by private companies, such as the Railway Company, the Dutch Iron Railway Company, the Dutch Rhine Railway Company and the Dutch Central Railway Company.
About twenty of the stations built in this period are protected under the Monuments Act.

From left to right: the stations at Groningen, Haarlem and Valkenburg.

From left to right: the stations at Zwolle, Baarn and Middelburg.

Haarlem Station (North Holland).

Tile picture in Haarlem Station.

Water-towers

There are water-towers all over the Netherlands and whether they are on the outskirts of a town or in the open countryside they stand out because of their distinctive shapes and varied styles of architecture.
They mark an important step in the history of public health: the supply of piped drinking-water to homes in the late nineteenth and early twentieth century.
Towns and areas with insufficient or bad drinking water were provided with pure water through pipes and as a result such infectious diseases as cholera and typhus became a thing of the past.
In order to ensure that there is sufficient pressure for the water to reach taps on the top floors of buildings, it is pumped from a purified water cooler below ground to a reservoir at the top of the water-tower. Naturally, nowadays more use is made of powerful pumps, especially in view of the many high-rise buildings.
The first water-tower in the Netherlands was built in 1856 in Den Helder but has since been demolished. About twenty years later towers were built at Scheveningen and Rotterdam.

Water-tower, Rotterdam (South Holland).

Collection, purification and storage of water

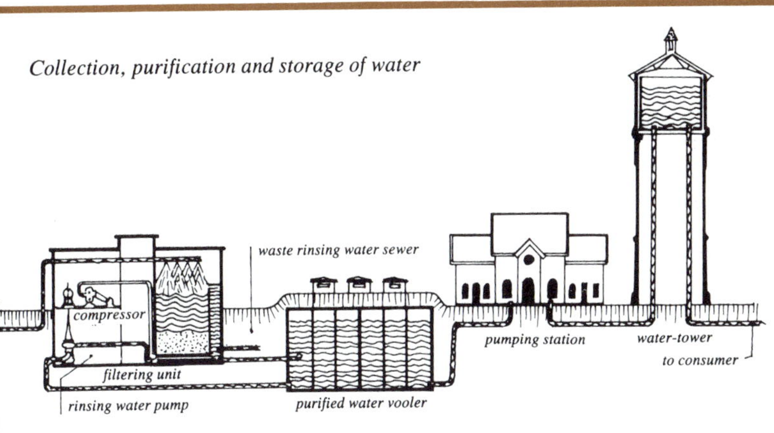

Water-tower, Woerden (South Holland).

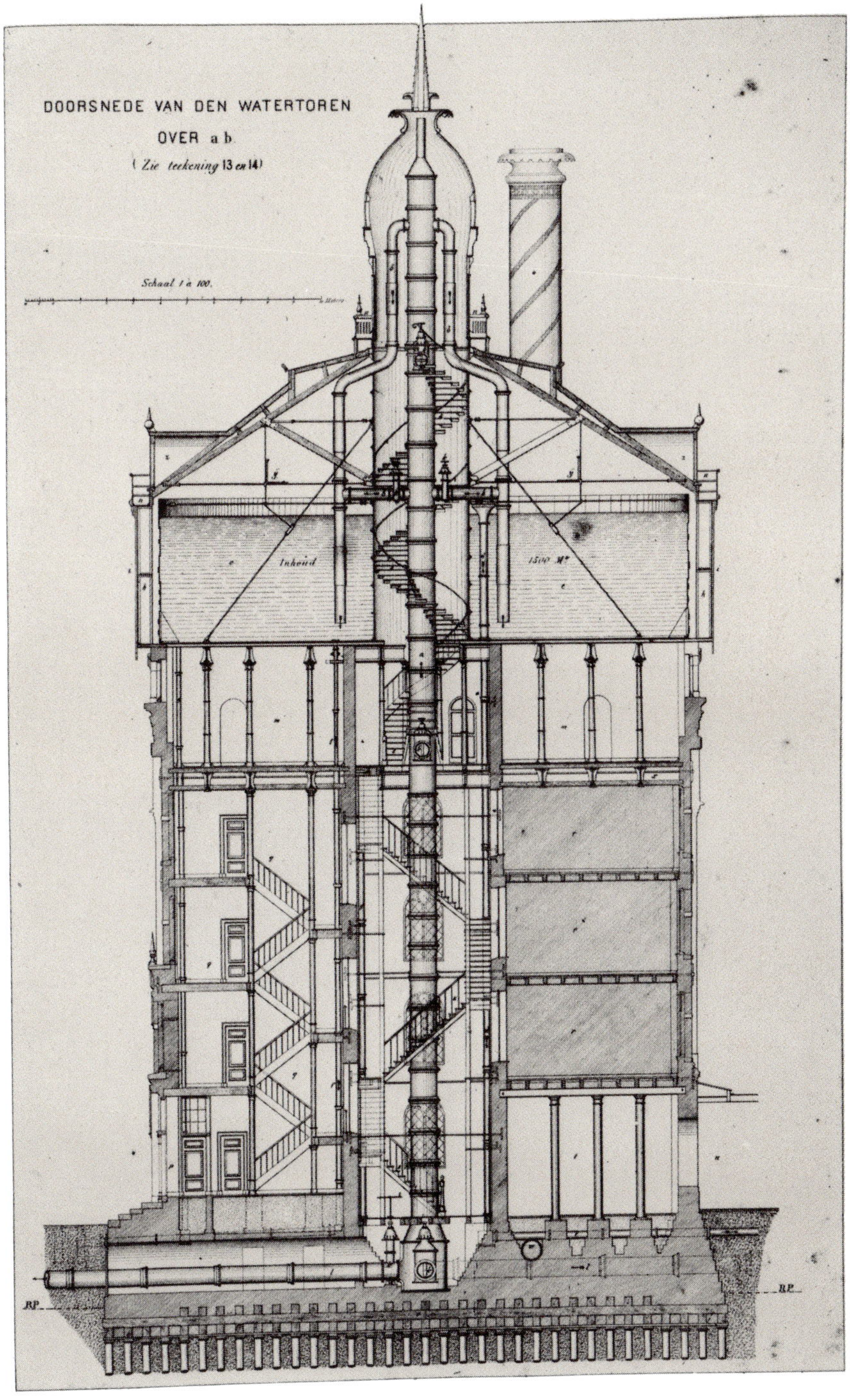

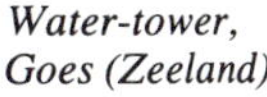

Water-tower, Goes (Zeeland).

Water-tower, Schoonhoven (Utrecht).

Cross section of water-tower, Rotterdam (South Holland).

Steam Pumping Stations

This section could have come directly after the chapter on windmills, since steam pumping stations have replaced windmills either wholly or partly.
A steam pumping station consists of a steam engine, pumps and water wheels and/or screws. A pump of this kind operates in exactly the same way as a windmill except that it is driven by steam pressure instead of wind. Because of the continuous supply of energy the pumping station has much greater potential. Steam pumping stations were built on a large scale between 1850 and 1920 for use in draining lakes and reclaiming land. In 1920 the Netherlands had more than 700 of these stations; only about 10 have survived, all of them protected under the Monuments Act.

Engine room, steam pumping station, Putten (Gelderland).

Steam pumping station, Medemblik (North Holland).

Steam pumping station, Nijkerk (Gelderland).

'De Vier Noorder Koggen', steam pumping station, Medemblik (North Holland).

'De Cruquius', steam pumping station, Haarlemmermeer (North Holland).

Lighthouses

Before sailors had the navigational equipment and instruments they have nowadays it was very difficult for them to recognize harbours or dangerous coastal waters whilst out at sea. Seamen's guides were largely filled with descriptions of the coastline, and of how it could be recognized by landmarks such as dunes, church towers, mills and high buildings. If a coast had few landmarks or none at all it was especially important to erect wooden or cast-iron constructions which could be sighted during the day-time and used for fires or lights to guide ships at night.

The oldest written record of lighthouses in the Netherlands dates from 1280 when the church at Brielle gave permission for two beacons to be placed at the mouth of the river Maas. The fires were originally fuelled with wood or straw and after 1600 with coal. Towards the end of the 18th century fires were gradually replaced by oil lamps with mirrors and lenses, and at the beginning of this century electric lighting took over.

Until the 19th century coastal lighting was limited to the stretches of coast near the principal ports and fishing harbours. However, owing to the enormous increase in shipping in the 19th century more coastal lighting had to be provided at fairly short notice. Between 1822 and 1863 five new brick lighthouses were built and a number of old lighthouses were rebuilt or modernized. About a dozen cast iron lighthouses were constructed between 1863 and 1899. With the odd exception all of them are still in operation.

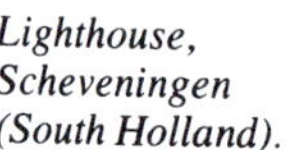

Lighthouse, Scheveningen (South Holland).

Lighthouse, IJmuiden (North Holland).

Brass plate of lighthouse, Vlieland (Friesland).

Lighthouse, West Terschelling (Friesland), aerial photograph.

Lighthouse lenses, Schiermonnikoog (Friesland).

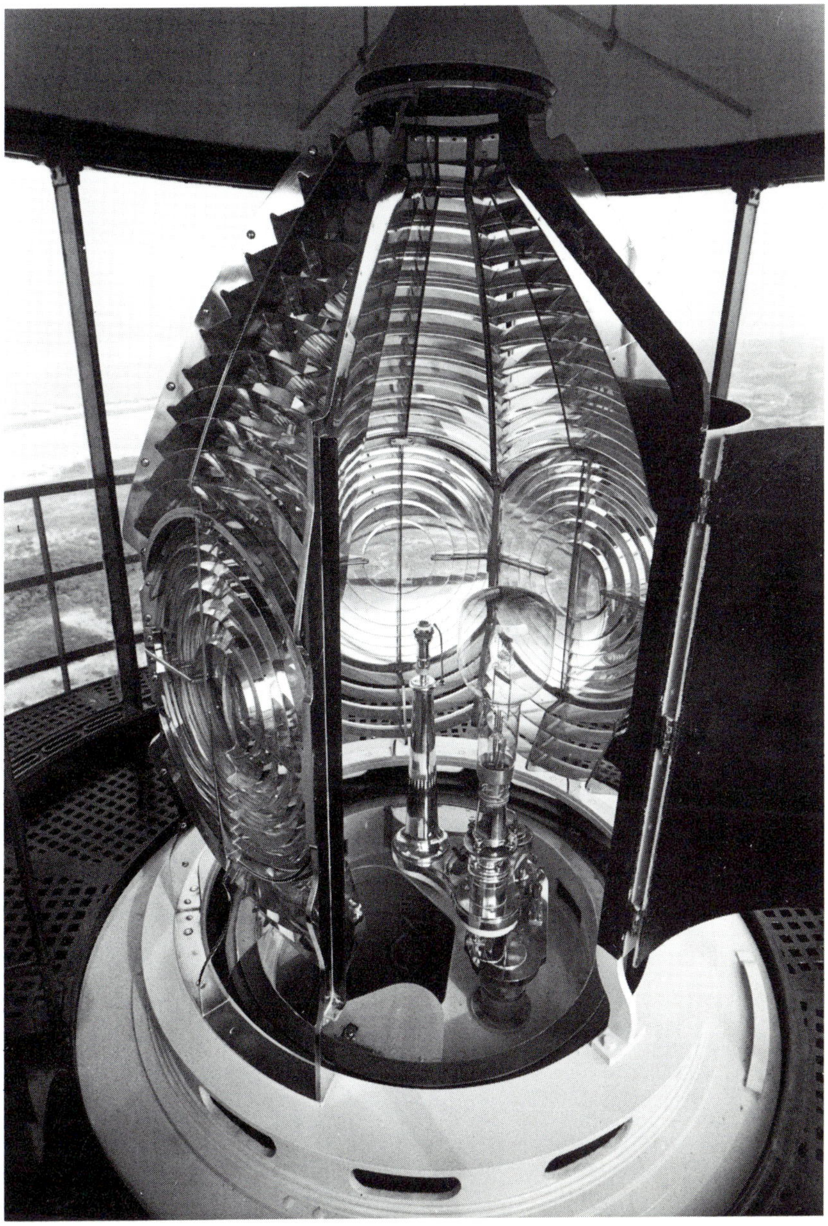

Literature

Town and villages

Fockema Andreae, Ter Kuile, Hekker, *Duizend jaar bouwen in Nederland* (A Thousand Years of Building in the Netherlands), Amsterdam 1957.
Van Voorden e.a., *Stads- en dorpsgezichten in Gelderland* (Towns and Villages in Gelderland), Zutphen 1975.
Kunstreisboek voor Nederland (Guide to Art in the Netherlands), Amsterdam 1977.
Monument en Samenleving: discussienota van de Raad van Europeese gemeenten (Monuments and the Community: discussion paper of the Council of European Municipalities), Maastricht 1974.

Dwelling Houses

R. Meischke & H. J. Zantkuil, *Het Nederlandse woonhuis van 1300-1800* (The Dutch House from 1300 to 1800), a commemorative publication of the Hendrick de Keyser Association, Haarlem 1969
H. J. Zantkuil, *Bouwen in Amsterdam* (Building in Amsterdam), nos. 1-18, Amsterdam 1973-1977
C. L. Temminck Groll, *Middeleeuwse stenen huizen te Utrecht* (Mediaeval Stone Houses in Utrecht), The Hague 1963
H. Janse & S. de Jong, *Houten huizen* (Wooden Houses), Zaltbommel 1970
H. Janse, *Vensters* (Windows), Nijmegen 1971
J. G. Wattes & J. A. Warners, *Amsterdamsche Bouwkunst en Stadsschoon 1306-1942* (Amsterdam Architecture and Urban Scenery), Amsterdam 1943
J. H. W. Leliman, *Het stadswoonhuis in Nederland gedurende de laatste 25 jaren* (Town Houses in the Netherlands over the past 25 years), The Hague 1920
G. Fanelli, *Moderne architectuur in Nederland, 1900-1940* (Modern Architecture in the Netherlands, 1900-1940), The Hague 1978
D. J. Grinberg, *Housing in the Netherlands 1900-1940,* Delft 1970
The volumes published to date in the series *Geïllustreerde Beschrijvingen van Geschiedenis en Kunst* (Illustrated Descriptions of Dutch Historical and Architectural Monuments) published by the State Commission on Monument Description
K. Sluyterman, *Huisraad en binnenhuis in Nederland in vroegere eeuwen* (Home furnishings and interiors in the Netherlands in former centuries), The Hague 1947, facsimile reprint 1975
W. van der Pluym, *Vijf eeuwen binnenhuis en meubels in Nederland, 1450-1950* (Five centuries of interiors and furniture in the Netherlands, 1450-1950), Amsterdam 1954
J. Schouten, *Stijlkamers in Nederland* (Period Rooms in the Netherlands), Amsterdam
'Kunstreisboek voor Nederland' (Guide to Art in the Netherlands), Amsterdam-Antwerp 1977

Castles and Country Houses

E. W. Moes and K. Sluyterman, *Nederlandse Kastelen en hun historie* (Dutch Castles and Their History), 3 volumes. Amsterdam, 1912-15. Description and history of a selected number of castles.
E. H. ter Kuile, *Kastelen en adellijke huizen* (Castles and Great Houses). No. 13 in the series, *De schoonheid van ons land,* Amsterdam 1954.
Ingrid W. L. Moerman, *Kastelen en hun bewoners* (Castles and Their Occupants). No. 9 in the Fibula Junior Series, Bussum, 1970. Largely about mediaeval fortified castles and the everyday lives of their occupants.
A. I. J. M. Schellart and T. de Vries, *Burchten en kastelen* (Fortresses and Castles). Wassenaar, 1974.
A. I. J. M. Schellart et al., *Kastelen* (Castles). Deventer, 1974.
A. I. J. M. Schellart et al., *Historische landhuizen* (Historic Country Houses), Deventer, 1974.
Nederlandse buitenplaatsen bedreigd? (Are Dutch Country Houses at Risk?). An illustrated guide to an exhibition of the same name held in Het Prinsenhof Museum, Delft, in 1972.
H. W. M. van der Wijck, *De Nederlandse buitenplaats* (Dutch Country Houses). Doctoral thesis composed mainly of articles by the author previously published in Dutch and foreign journals. Utrecht, 1974.
C. H. C. A. van Sypesteyn, *Oud-Nederlandse tuinkunst* (The Traditional Art of Gardening in the Netherlands), The Hague, 1910.
Anna G. Bienfait, *Oude Hollandsche tuinen,* (Old Dutch Gardens). With a separate volume of illustrations. The Hague, 1932.
J. T. P. Bijhouwer, *Nederlandsche tuinen en buitenplaatsen* (Dutch Gardens and Country Estates), third impression. Amsterdam, 1946.
C. Taudin Chabot, ed., *Wegwijzer naar Hollandsche tuinen* (Guide to Dutch Gardens). Obtainable from the Netherlands Castles Society, Van Ostadelaan 43, Muiderberg.

Churches

Andreae, Fockema-, S. J., E. H. ter Kuile and R. C. Hekker, *Duizend jaar bouwen in Nederland* (A thousand years of building in the Netherlands) 2 parts, Amsterdam, 1948-1958.
Janse, H., *De Lotgevallen der Nederlandse Kerkgebouwen* (The changing Fortunes of Dutch churches). Zaltbommel, 1969.
Kuile, Dr E. H. ter, *De Romaanse Kerkbouwkunst in de Nederlanden.* (Romanesque Church Architecture in the Low Countries). Zutphen, 1975.
Kunstreisboek voor Nederland, (Guide to Art in the Netherlands), Amsterdam/Antwerp, 1977.
Mönnich, Dr C. W., *De kerk in het midden; kerken, hoven, kapellen, langs onze velden en wegen* (The Church in our midst; churches, farmhouses and chapels along the highways and byways), Zutphen, 1976.
Ozinga, M. D., *De protestantse kerkenbouw in Nederland van de Hervorming tot den Franschen tijd,* (Protestant churches in the Netherlands from the Reformation to Napoleon). Amsterdam, 1929.
Rosenberg, H. P. R., *De 19de eeuwse kerkelijke bouwkunst in Nederland* (Nineteenth-century church architecture in the Netherlands). The Hague, 1972.
Steensma, R., *Vroomheid in hout en steen; middeleeuwse kerken in Noord-Nederland* (Piety in wood and stone; mediaeval church architecture in the Northern Netherlands). Baarn, 1976.
Steensma, a.o., *Oude Nederlandse kerken, langs de --,* (A tour of old Dutch churches) 14 parts. Baarn, 1966-1977.

Farmhouses

R. C. Hekker: *De ontwikkeling van de boerderijvormen in Nederland* (The development of farmhouses in the Netherlands), in Duizend jaar bouwen II (A Thousand Years of Construction II); Amsterdam, 1957, pp. 195-316.
Historische boerderijtypen (Historical Farmhouses) in Atlas van Nederland blad X-1 (Atlas of the Netherlands, part X-1) with a note by R. C. Hekker; The Hague, 1973.
Information on Dutch rural architecture, 5 folders of survey sketches and explanations; Arnhem, Netherlands Open Air Museum, 1961-1971.
Jaarverslagen Stichting Historisch Boerderij-onderzoek (Annual Reports, Association for research on historical farmhouses, Arnhem).
P. J. 't Hooft: *Nederlandse boerderijen,* Heemschutserie deel 9 (Dutch Farmhouses, Heemschut series part 9); Amsterdam, 1941.
Evert Zandstra: *Shell boerderijengids* (The Shell Guide to Farms); Shell, 1964.
Kees Post, Ger Dekkers and A. A. C. Maaskant: *Oude boerderijen* (Old Farmhouses); Deventer, 1969.
Kees Post: *Het boerenhuis in Nederland* (The Dutch Farmhouse), Triangel series; The Hague, 1975.
S. J. van der Molen: *Langs Frieslands oude boerderijen* (A Tour of Friesland's Old Farmhouses); Baarn, 1974.
Jan Jans: *Landelijke bouwkunst in Oost-Nederland* (Rural Architecture in the East of the Netherlands); Enschede, 1967.
L. Brandt Buys: *De landelijke bouwkunst in Hollands Noorderkwartier* (Rural Architecture in the North of Holland); Arnhem, Stichting Historisch Boerderij-onderzoek 1974.

Mills

J. C. Hoornenborg: Molenbehoud in Nederland, civiele verdediging en romantiek (The preservation of mills in the Netherlands, civil defence and romance), in: *Tijdschrift Civiele Verdediging* No. 3, April-May 1973
E. Smit: *Zorg voor de molenbiotoop'* (Conservation of the mill environment), Heemschut 1973
A. Bicker Caarten: *Waar 't om gaat; tien jaar strijd om het molenbehoud in Rijnland*

(The issue: ten years of campaigning for mill preservation in Rijnland), Leiden 1969
A. Bicker Caarten: *De molen in ons volksleven'* (The windmill in popular Dutch tradition), Leiden 1958
K. Boonenburg: *De Windmolens* (Windmills), Amsterdam 1949
H. A. Visser: *Zwaaiende wieken* (Turning sails), Amsterdam 1946
F. Stockhuysen: *Molens* (Mills), Bussum 1961

Provincial mill books
Groninger Molens (Groningen mills), Groningen 1958
Molens in Friesland (Mills in Friesland), Leeuwarden 1971
Molens in Overijssel (Mills in Overijssel), Zwolle 1972
Gelders Molenboek (The Gelderland Mill Book), Zutphen 1968
Molenboek provincie Utrecht (The Mill Book of the Province of Utrecht), Utrecht 1972
Noord-Hollands molenboek (The North Holland Mill Book), Haarlem 1964
Zuid-Hollands molenboek (The South Holland Mill Book), Alphen a/d Rijn 1965
De molens van Zeeland (The Mills of Zeeland), Middelburg 1973
De Brabantse molens (The Brabant Mills), Helmond 1973
Molens in Limburg (Mills in Limburg), Maastricht 1957

List of addresses

Ministry of Cultural Affairs, Recreation and Social Work, Steenvoordelaan 370, 2284 EH Rijswijk (ZH) or Winston Churchilllaan 362, 2284 JN Rijswijk (ZH), telephone (0)70-949233/949293

Rijksdienst voor de Monumentenzorg (Department for the Preservation of Monuments and Historic Buildings), Broederplein 41, 3703 CD Zeist (P.O. Box 1001, 3700 BA Zeist), telephone (0)3404-28122.

Rijksdienst voor het Oudheidkundig Bodemonderzoek (Archaeological Research Department), Kleine Haag 2, 3811 HE Amersfoort, telephone (0)33-12648.

National Organisations

Stichting Nationale Contactcommissie Monumentenbescherming (NCM) (National Coordinating Committee for the Protection of Monuments).
There are over 600 national, regional or local organizations in the Netherlands that are concerned with the protection of monuments and historic buildings. Much important work is done by the large number of purely local ones. The NCM endeavours to help these organizations keep in touch with one another and to present their case – that of the voluntary organizations – to official bodies. The board of the NCM includes representations of the organizations mentioned below and of the Amsterdamse Maatschappij van Stadsherstel (urban renewal projects), the ANWB (Royal Dutch Touring Club) and NIROV (Institute of Land-use Planning and Housing).
Address: St. Antoniesbreestraat 69, 1011 HB Amsterdam, telephone (0)20-277706.

The following organizations accept private members and supply a wide range of information on monuments or historic buildings.

Heemschut League
The League was founded in 1911 and is concerned with protecting Holland's heritage of monuments and historic buildings. Its primary objective is to combat the increasing disfigurement of towns, villages and the Dutch countryside by bringing pressure to bear on private individuals or official bodies. The League has branches in each province and a team of technical advisors. It publishes a monthly journal entitled 'Heemschut' containing articles on the protection of monuments and on the League's activities.
Address: Korenmetershuis, Nieuwezijds Kolk 28, 1012 PV Amsterdam, telephone (0)20-225292.

Royal Netherlands Archaeological Society
The members of the Society include students and amateurs as well as professional architects and archaeologists. It aims to further knowledge in its field by producing specialist publications and organising seminars rather than by undertaking campaigns on specific issues.

The society also tries to develop new initiatives and to give critical assessments of the policies of official bodies and private organizations. It produces a bulletin five times a year.
Address: De Poorterstraat 22, 2597 CS The Hague, telephone (0)70-240315.

'De Hollandsche Molen' (The Dutch Mill Society)
The society is concerned first and foremost with the conservation of windmills and watermills, which it does by organising publicity, promoting restoration, giving technical advice and, in certain cases, by purchasing mills. Members receive a copy of the society's journal and can take part in excursions. The society works in close collaboration with a large number of local societies, such as the Gilde van Vrijwillige Molenaars, P.O. Box 71119, Amsterdam, whose members work in their spare time to help keep old mills turning, and the Stichting Ambachtelijk Korenmolenaarsgilde, which tries to keep the traditional craft of the miller alive by preserving corn mills in full working order. 'De Hollandsche Molen' can provide information on the various societies for mill enthusiasts throughout the country.
Address: Prins Hendrikkade 108-114, 1011 AK Amsterdam, telephone (0)20-238703.

Hendrick de Keyser Society
The society was set up in 1918 by a number of people in Amsterdam who were concerned about the disappearance of historic buildings in the city centre. The society works for the conservation of historic premises throughout the country; it usually buys them with a view to restoration and subsequent letting. It now has over 220 premises in 59 towns and villages in the Netherlands.
Address: Herengracht 284, 1016 BX Amsterdam, telephone (0)20-249755.

Netherlands Castles and Country Houses Society
The society, which was founded in 1945, works for the preservation of castles, historic country houses and other buildings in the Netherlands, in the interests of the national heritage or the environment. Its activities include organising publicity, promoting visits to castles and historic country houses in the Netherlands, disseminating information on castles for both specialists and non-specialists, encouraging excavations and organising excursions.
Address: Kuluutsheuvel 32, 5825 BE Overloon, telephone (0)4788-565.

Menno van Coehoorn Society
The society was founded in 1932 and is named after the Netherlands' most famous military architect. It is concerned with the preservation of fortifications that have outlived their military usefulness but which are of historical or artistic value or are important features of the landscape. The society produces reports, organises excursions, publishes an annual journal and organises campaigns when remains of former military sites are threatened with damage or destruction.
Address: P.O. Box 110, 5060 AC Oisterwijk, telephone (0)4242-2346.

'Het Behouden Huis' Association
This is an association of locally-based organizations concerned with the restoration of historic dwelling houses, which constitute a major component of the national heritage and one that is crucial to the appearance of many inner-city areas. There are organizations for the restoration of houses in every town of any size. The association advises member organizations and also represents them in talks with the authorities on matters involving finance, taxation etc.
Address: Sloterkade 21, 1058 HE Amsterdam, telephone (0)20-172735.

National Organizations outside the NCM

Society for the Preservation of Nature Research in the Netherlands
The society is the largest private nature conservation organization in the country,

with over 250,000 members. Its main interest is the conservation and management of areas of natural or scientific importance. Over the years it has acquired over 33,000 hectares of land as well as a large amount of farmland of special interest and hundreds of buildings (castles, mills, farmhouses, country houses etc.). The society's most important task is to save threatened areas of natural beauty by means of purchase and management.
Its members receive a magazine, entitled 'Natuurbehoud', four times a year and a handbook containing brief descriptions of the areas of natural beauty in the Netherlands. Address: Noordeinde 60, 1243 JJ 's-Graveland, telephone (0)35-62004.

Farmhouses
Information on farmhouses may be obtained from Stichting Boerderijonderzoek, Schelmseweg 89, 6816 SJ Arnhem, telephone (0)85-45065.

Churches
There are various local and regional organizations that are concerned with the preservation of interesting churches. Information may be obtained from the NCM (address above).

Acknowledgments

The Rijksdienst voor Monumentenzorg and the publisher would like to thank the following organisations and individuals for their kind permission to reproduce the photographs in this book:
Aerophoto Eelde: 57 below; ANWB 32 above; J. Bergsma, Schoonhoven: 20 above left; A. Bicker Caarten: 126 below, 128 above left; Centraal Reprobureau, Assen: 15 above; © Gerrit Rietveld 1982 c/o Beeldrecht, Amsterdam: 49; Frequin Photo's, Voorburg: 82; Gem. Archiefdienst, Maastricht: 29 boven; KLM Aerocarto bv, Schiphol: 11 below, 12 above, below, 13 above, below, 14 below, 15 centre right, below, 21 below, 27 below, 52 below, 58 below; H. Kortland, Zeist: 17 above, centre left, 21 above, 24 below, 29 below right, 32 below, 56 below, 66 below left, above right, 67, 70, 74 above, 78; B. P. Koster: 128 right; J. Kroon, Lelystad: 119 below, 122 above left, 123 below right, 126 above left, 127 above, below; Kunsthistorisch Instituut, Utrecht: 71 below; Openlucht Museum, Arnhem: 106, below, 108 above, 109, 110 below, 111, 112 below, 113; Prov. Planologische Dienst, Arnhem: 17 below; R. Steensma: 75; Stichting Kastelen Documentatie, Muiderberg: (G. Dekkers) 53 above, 57 above, 66 below; Ver. 'Hollandsche Molen', Amsterdam: 114, 118 above, centre right, 119 above right, 122 above right, below, 123 above, 126 above right, 127 left.

Index of places

Page numbers in italics refer to illustrations